Davenport Pottery and Porcelain 1794-1887

A representative group of colourful Davenport pottery and porcelain ware from the author's collection.

DAVENPORT POTTERY AND PORCELAIN 1794-1887

T. A. Lockett

David & Charles: Newton Abbot

UNIFORM WITH THIS BOOK
Blue and White Transfer Ware 1780-1840 by A. W. Coysh

For Isabel

ISBN 0 7153 5681 X

Set in 10 on 11 point Plantin by C. E. Dawkins (Typesetters) Ltd., SE1
and printed in Great Britain
Latimer Trend & Company Limited Whitstable
for David & Charles (Publishers) Limited

CONTENTS

ACKNOWLEDGEMENTS

A great many people have generously assisted me in the preparation of this book, far too many to name individually. To three such my debt of gratitude is considerable: To Reginald Haggar who has consistently encouraged me and supplied many valuable items of information; to Mr Arnold Mountford, Director of the Hanley Museum Stoke-on-Trent, I am immensely grateful, for it was he who most generously directed my attention to the *Foxley* and *Wood* papers, and he has continued to assist me in many ways. Thirdly, it is difficult to overstate the help of Mr Geoff Taylor who has so skilfully and patiently photographed my own pieces and prepared the lay-out for the illustrations. His co-operation has been invaluable.

For help in directing my attention to Davenport wares or assisting me with documentary material, I am especially indebted to Mrs Elizabeth Adams. Also to Mrs A. Atterbury, Mrs J. Busby, Mrs A. Capon, Mrs Angela Cox, Mr A. H. Dodson, Mrs J. L. Davenport, Mr and Mrs A. A. Eaglestone, Mr N. Emery, Mrs Hilary Evans, Mr and Mrs J. G. Evans, Mr J. K. des Fontaines FRSA, Mr D. L. Jones, Mrs M. Newton, Mr M. Palmer, Mr G. H. Pinhorn, Mr A. Shaw-Wright of the Hereford County Record Office, Mr A. Shelley of Allied English Potteries, Mr A. Thomas and Mr L. Whiter.

I am also indebted to the following who assisted me with photographs and information about their wares which are here reproduced by the courtesy of their owners, and are acknowledged in the captions: Mr Geoffrey de Bellaigue, Deputy Surveyor of the Queen's Works of Art, Miss J. Hoos and Miss J. Langton who provided information on the Royal dessert service, which is illustrated by Gracious permission of Her Majesty the Queen; Mr R. J. Charleston and Miss D. Griffiths of the Victoria and Albert Museum; Mr J. K. Crellin of the Wellcome Institute of the History of Medicine; Mr G. A. Elliott of the Hanley Museum Stoke-on-Trent: Mrs A. M. James of the City of Liverpool Museum; Mr F. J. Laws of the Castle Museum Nottingham, Sotheby & Co, and Mr Hartley Asquith, Mrs E. Blatch, Mrs Elizabeth Collard of Montreal, Mr and Mrs D. W. Crompton, Mr and Mrs J. K. des Fontaines, Mr G. A. Godden FRSA, and Mr. Brian Smith To all these, and many others, my thanks.

NOTES ON THE ILLUSTRATIONS

(a) The pieces illustrated are acknowledged to their owners by whose courtesy they are published here. Where no such acknowledgment is made the item is from the author's collection.

(b) The mark on each piece is indicated by a number (No 1-24) which refers to the corresponding mark illustrated on p 111.

(c) As wide a spectrum of wares as possible has been illustrated from the magnificence of the royal service to the simplicity of cheap earthenwares. Thus the range of the factory's output is outlined, though far from comprehensively covered.

By the same author
The Rockingham Pottery (with A. A. Eaglestone)

INTRODUCTION AND REFERENCES

The past decade has witnessed a considerable growth in active research into the history and production of English potteries. Many gaps in our knowledge—especially of the nineteenth century potters—have recently been filled. This present work is a further contribution to these studies.

The firm of Davenport of Longport, Staffordshire has, considering its size and contemporary importance, been much neglected. Largely this has been because of a lack of documents and other information. To some extent this is still the case. Few documents have come down to us about certain periods of the factory's history. Indeed, the present study would not have been attempted were it not for the *Foxley Collection*, generously deposited in the Hereford County Record Office in 1960 by the late Major J. L. and Mrs Davenport of Mansel Lacy, which cover the period 1812-35, and the *Wood* papers (1875-1887) in the Hanley Museum collection.

Before these two valuable sources became available the student had only some older secondary works of mixed merit (see References). No subsequent modern works have greatly added to our knowledge of the history of the concern.

Turning to the wares, the situation is similar. No major collection of Davenport is known to the author. There are small representative collections in the Museums at Hanley, Liverpool, the Victoria and Albert and the British Museum. The Sadler Collection housed at Myott's factory in Cobridge, contains several dozen Davenport items, and a handful of pieces may be seen in most ceramic collections such as those at the Harris Museum, Preston, and the Castle Museum, Nottingham. Specific and detailed reference is made to wares in these collections in the text. Thus by comparison with Spode, Rockingham, Minton, or in fact with almost any major nineteenth century pottery, the lack of a corpus of wares for comparative study is disappointing. This presents a challenge to the student and the collector.

The Davenport enterprise flourished for nearly a century. There is still much to be discovered both about the narrative history of the factory and about its wares. It is hoped that this first study of what was one of the country's largest potteries will encourage others to turn their attention to a neglected area of research. Davenport wares are increasingly sought after; they are still comparatively plentiful, though they are becoming more expensive as each year passes. The best of the pots of John Davenport and his successors, whether made for the home market or for export to America, Canada, India or other foreign places, can stand comparison with any of the products of their more-esteemed contemporaries. Moreover, as they span the period from the death of Josiah Wedgwood to the dawn of art nouveau, they offer a wide spectrum of stylistic and aesthetic interest.

REFERENCES

The books listed below are all referred to in the text. When this happens the author's name only will be used, followed by the number of the relevant page or plate. Where the same author is responsible for more than one book an abbreviated title will be used. References to journals, magazines and newspaper articles are given in full in the text.

In the historical section, substantial reference has been made to the following early publications:

Jewitt, Llewellynn *The Ceramic Art of Great Britain* (2 Vols 1878)

Miller, M. H. *Olde Leek* (2 Vols 1891)

Scarrett, W. *Old Times in the Potteries* (1906; 1969)

Shaw, C. (An Old Potter) *When I was a Child* (1903; 1969)

Shaw, Simeon *A History of the Staffordshire Potteries* (1829; 1970)

Sleigh, J. *A History of the Ancient Parish of Leek in Staffordshire* (1883)

Ward, John *A History of the Borough of Stoke-upon-Trent* (1843; 1969)

Wedgwood, J. C. *Staffordshire Pottery and its History* (1912)

Other text references relate to the following:

Adams, P. L. W. *John Henry Clive* (1947)

Barton, R. M. *A History of the Cornish China-clay Industry* (1966)

Bemrose, G. V. *Nineteenth Century English Pottery and Porcelain* (1952)

Collard, E. *Nineteenth Century Pottery and Porcelain in Canada* (1967)

Coysh, A. W. *Blue and White Transfer Ware 1780-*

1840 (1970)
Crellin, J. K. *Medical Ceramics in the Wellcome Institute* (1969)
Eaglestone, A. A. and Lockett, T. A. *The Rockingham Pottery* (1964; 1967)
Evans, W. *The Art and History of the Potting Business* (1846; reprinted in *Journal of Ceramic History* No 3, 1970)
Godden, G. A. *Encyclopaedia of British Pottery and Porcelain Marks* (1964) (abbreviated in text to Godden, *Marks*); *An Illustrated Encyclopaedia of British Pottery and Porcelain* (1966) (abbreviated in text to Godden, *Encyclopaedia*); *Coalport and Coalbrookdale Porcelains* (1970); *Masons Patent Ironstone China* (1970); *Minton Pottery and Porcelain of the First Period 1793-1850* (1968); *Victorian Porcelain* (1961)
Gunnis, R. *Dictionary of British Sculptors 1660-1851* (1968)
Haggar, R. G. *The Masons of Lane Delph* (1952)
Hillier, B. *The Turners of Lane End* (1965)
Hobson, R. L. *Catalogue of the Collection of English Porcelain in the British Museum* (1905)
Holgate, D. *New Hall and its Imitators* (1970)
Little, W. L. *Staffordshire Blue* (1969)
Mankowitz, W. and Haggar, R. G. *The Concise Encyclopaedia of English Pottery and Porcelain* (1957)
Moore, N. H. *The Old China Book* (1946 edition)
Owen, H. *The Staffordshire Potter* (1906; 1970)
Rhead, G. W. and F. A. *Staffordshire Pots and Potters* (1906)
Rice, D. G. *Rockingham Pottery and Porcelain* (1971)
Schinn, C. and D. *Victorian Parian China* (1971)
Smith, A. *Liverpool Herculaneum Pottery* (1971)
Thomas, Dr J. *The Rise of the Staffordshire Potteries* (1971)
Towner, D. C. *English Cream-coloured Earthenware* (1957)
Victoria County History of Staffordshire Vol II and Vol VIII (abbreviated in text to *VCH*)
Warburton, W. H. *A History of Trade Union Organisation in the North Staffordshire Potteries* (1931)
Whiter, L. *Spode* (1970)

PART ONE: FAMILY AND FIRM

Fifty Years of Potting (1785-c 1835)
John Davenport

According to Ward, the first pottery erected in Longport was the premises of John Brindley, built in 1773, appropriately enough on the banks of the canal in whose development his more famous brother James had played such a prominent part. It was this Pottery called Unicorn Bank which John Davenport purchased and enlarged in 1794 (Jewitt gives 1793), and so began his career as an independent master-potter and the founder of a great firm and a considerable fortune. At this date he was twenty-nine years old.

Information about John Davenport's early life is very sparse. The most reliable narrative is presented by Sleigh. He notes that John Davenport was born 29 September 1765 in a house in Derby Street, Leek. His family were of yeoman stock, and Sleigh gives a family pedigree traced back to 1585. When John was only six his father died and the boy had to be taken away from school. Shortly afterwards he was put to work with a Mr Lucas whose business failed, involving the loss of his mother's 'small fortune'. He then went to work in Newcastle in the bank of Mr Kinnersley, and here he remained until 1785 when at the age of twenty he joined Thomas Wolfe at a pottery adjoining Mintons in Stoke (G. W. and F. A. Rhead, p 289). Three years later he became Wolfe's partner at the Islington China Works in Liverpool (Mankowitz and Haggar, p 67). This arrangement lasted until 1794 when Davenport purchased Brindley's Longport Pottery and Miles Mason succeeded him as Wolfe's partner in Liverpool.

This is the sum of our knowledge of John Davenport's early career. There is no record of the price he paid Brindley, but the obvious inference is that he had prospered since he left the bank to become Wolfe's partner.

In its early years, in common with most Staffordshire potteries of the period, the Longport pottery produced the normal range of wares then fashionable, all of which are discussed in full later. Shortly after John Davenport began his independent career, two important events took place which, between them, marked a new stage of development in industrial pottery. In 1795 Josiah Wedgwood died. This event seemed to symbolise the end of the first and most exciting era in the industry's development. Davenport's links with Josiah I are, as far as we know, tenuous. He is, however, recorded as being associated with Josiah Wedgwood II, John and George Rogers, William Adams, the New Hall company and others totalling eighteen Staffordshire firms in a Potter's Clay Company which in 1796 was granted a lease of certain setts of ball clay in the Isle of Purbeck (R. M. Barton, p 36). Davenport cannot have remained unaffected by the business methods associated with Josiah I and, undoubtedly, imitated Wedgwood creamware patterns.

The advent of the next period in the industry's growth was significantly heralded by the development of bone china by Josiah Spode. It is recorded that John Davenport visited France prior to 1800 to enquire about porcelain-making methods, the likelihood of this and the general story of the exploitation of Spode's innovations are more fully discussed on p 72.

Davenport had begun his independent career at the beginning of a period of war with France. The war was to last with little remission until 1815; and, like those of his fellow potters, Davenport's exports were affected. His patriotism clearly was not, for during the 'invasion scare' of 1803, *Major* Davenport (according to Ward) raised four companies of the Volunteer Corps each of eighty rank and file. 'This gallant corps Mr Davenport brought into a high state of discipline.'

By this time, the Davenport enterprise had grown and clearly prospered. In 1801 (again according to Ward), the manufacture of flint glass was begun at Longport. This was an unusual departure for a potter, and an aspect of the firm's activities which continued until the closure. Glassmaking, of course is beyond the scope of the present work, but it is worth recording that by 1805 the glass business too was flourishing and being operated by Davenport, Kinnersley & Grafton. Thomas Kinnersley, who was also to become a partner in the pottery business, was a Newcastle lawyer and business man. In 1826 Simeon Shaw notes him as being the owner of the Kidsgrove and Whitehill collieries, 'very extensive and productive'. His residence was at Clough Hall. Grafton was a practical glassmaker and the glassworks manager.

Though no records exist to prove the point, it is manifest that in his first dozen years of independent operation John Davenport had made a great deal of money. He owned a pottery producing both earthenware and porcelain and a glassworks. He is also recorded as being the owner of the Cliff Bank Pottery, Stoke, formerly worked by John Harrison, but advertised and sold to John Davenport in 1804. He then leased the premises to William Adams (VCH, Vol VIII, p 202). If further evidence of his standing is needed, the visit of HRH the Prince of Wales in 1806 is sufficient accolade. During the second week of September 1806, the Prince of Wales and his brother the Duke of Clarence (the future William IV) were staying at Trentham Park, having previously visited the premises of Spode (see Whiter, pp 30-31) and Etruria:

> On Saturday morning the Illustrious Party proceeded from Trentham to view Messrs Davenport's Manufactory of Ornamental Pottery & China Wares, and Messrs Kinnersley, Davenport and Graftons Glass Works at Longport. . . . On the fine Specimens of Porcelain, produced at this Manufactory His Royal Highness observed, *that he considered them in texture and execution equal to the Old Seve, that the Colours and Paintings did great credit to the Artists, and that he should feel proud in exhibiting them to his Foreign Visitors, to shew them, that their boasted superiority was now nearly, if not altogether, at an end.* His Royal Highness ordered Services of several of the finest and most valuable kinds:— Of the Ornamental parts of the Manufactory, His Royal Highness was pleased to say that the Vases, Urns &c in point of execution and ornament were Unique in their kinds, and gave orders for a collection of the most beautiful and highly finished Specimens. (*Staffordshire Advertiser*, 20 September 1806.)

The premises which HRH visited were situated to the north-west of Trubshaw Cross between Davenport Street (as it now is) and the canal. The entrance to the works, which was of three storeys, had a central arch and was surmounted by a pointed niche, this was flanked by two projecting bays. Nearby was a brick-built three-storied house of five bays which like the re-built factory dated from the late 1790s. This was the master-potter's residence and was for many years the Longport home of John Davenport. Photographs of the two buildings are reproduced in *VCH*, Vol VIII, opposite p 172.

Following the royal visit a three-sided close of terraced cottages was erected. They had small front gardens, and the central pediment was dated 1807. These cottages, near to the site of the future Longport railway station, were built for the Davenport's employees, and were named Prince's Square (see *VCH*, Vol VIII, p 137).

Meanwhile the French Wars continued and the constraints placed upon trade by Napoleon's Continental System though obviously irksome did not retard the continued expansion of the firm. In 1807 we learn from a Memorandum from Thomas Byerley in London to the Wedgwood works at Etruria that 'Davenport has taken the Shakespeare Gallery for an exhibition room of his glass, E'ware and China. I am not at all frightened of this . . .' (quoted in E. Meteyard, *A Group of Englishmen*, 1871, p 338). This is the earliest reference to a London showroom.

In 1810, or thereabouts, a large earthenware manufactory at Newport was purchased. Formerly the property of Walter Daniel, it had been built in 1795 and (according to Mankowitz and Haggar) advertised for sale in 1804. This was an important acquisition and henceforth much of the firm's output of earthenware came from the Newport works.

It is apparent from the earliest letter in the *Foxley Collection* that at this time (13 November 1812) John Davenport was in partnership with his cousin James, though there is no evidence of when this partnership was entered into (*Foxley*, B47/IVD/1. *Note:* All the *Foxley* letters bear the prefix notation B47/IVD. To avoid repetition, the number only will be cited in future references). Furthermore, by 1812 a warehouse and saleroom had been established in Liverpool—its date of origin is not known though it may have been of recent foundation in 1812. James Davenport writes: 'As to the General business here, the En'ware department is done as well as it can be by Fynney. . . .' He is less satisfied with the glass business (*Foxley*, 1). The Liverpool agency was a further addition to John Davenport's already considerable business holdings.

Perhaps the most clear evidence that John Davenport was a truly successful master-potter was provided during the following year 1813 when he entered the ranks of the landed gentry. Sleigh records that the Westwood Estate, Leek, was purchased 'on 19-20 March 1813 of the Hon W'm Booth-Grey of Duffryn for £15,500.' The boy who had left Needhams School, Leek, 'at a tender age' because of his widowed mother's poor financial condition, had made his mark as a manufacturer, and now at the age of forty-eight had become a country gentleman. John Davenport was to live at Westwood, on and off, until his death there in 1848, but periodically he seems to have been uneasy about his adopted role. On 26 January 1831, writing to his son Henry who had tried to persuade him to return from London, he observes:

> As to my residence at Westwood I know that you would not recommend it only that you conceive it would result to my advantage—but I see no advantage myself—either in comfort or saving—and it would have been well for us all if I had never seen it—You see what the introduction of Game Cocks &c has done for us—which we should never have seen but at Westwood and you know what our trade has suffered by the attraction it afforded to affairs of Sports rather than business. I am speaking of myself & others but the observation could be applied to you . . . (*Foxley*, 62).

These doubts were in the future; in 1813 he would have had no misgivings.

Two years later in 1815 the long Napoleonic Wars ended. For John Davenport this opened up the prospect of renewed commercial intercourse with the markets of Europe so difficult to penetrate in wartime. He celebrated the occasion as Ward and C. Shaw inform us, with a procession of his workpeople who walked from Longport to Burslem, 'with a band of music which was connected with the works'. Davenport headed the victory parade along with the works manager James Mawdesley. They both wore glass hats specially made for the occasion and carried Davenport-glass walking sticks.

It is at this point in the narrative that the *Foxley* papers provide us with abundant evidence of the development of the firm over the next twenty years. Three themes predominate amidst the general story of expansion: John Davenport's detailed knowledge of pot-making which can best be dealt with when the wares are discussed in detail; Davenport's managerial flair and drive which was allied to personal intolerance and irascibility, and the great preoccupation of the firm with the export market.

On this latter point, there can be no doubt that the opening up of trade in the post-war period led to fierce competition. Wedgwood's were perhaps not the force they had been under Josiah I, but a host of other competitiors led by Spode and Masons strove to sell their wares. An indication of the tactics employed even in the home trade is conveyed in a letter from Child & Co the Edinburgh dealers to John Davenport, dated 12 January 1818:

> At last the Masons have opened out their *Forty H'hds* Stoneware and China here, and are selling by Auction, which circumstance of course for ever closes our Account with them. We fear it will, in some degree, injure our demand, but we must do the best we can, relying upon your support, for our mutual interest. . . . Can you get us anything in ware from Masons to match up. To avoid suspicion they might be sent to Liverpool, from thence by sea to Glasgow & readdressed.
>
> We fear it is Masons intention to have a permanent Connection here with an auctioneer. If so we must devise some plan for opposing them. . . . (*Foxley*, 2. See also p 60).

Mason's practice of selling by auction—details of which are given in both Reginald Haggar's and Geoffrey Godden's books on the factory—was much deplored by other manufacturers, who had either warehouses or agency arrangements with local china dealers in London, Edinburgh and elsewhere. They strongly objected to the Masons flooding the local market with their wares. For the local china dealers the situation was even worse. Thus it was a combination of this fierce home competition and the renewed export opportunities which increasingly directed Davenport's attention overseas.

As was normal in those days he recruited his own family to occupy managerial positions both at home and abroad. He had married in 1795 Diana Smart Ward, the daughter of Michael Ward of Newcastle. They had five children before her death in 1811. The eldest child was Elizabeth, born in 1795, who married Sir John Bent of Liverpool. The second child and eldest son John Davenport II somewhat strangely did not follow his father into the potting business. According to Miller he went to Worcester College Oxford and was called to the Bar in 1828. He seems to have spent much of his time at Westwood. 'He occupied his leisure moments in literary pursuits', and eventually purchased the Foxley estate in Herefordshire to which he and his family moved. John Davenport's other two sons played a prominent part in the management of the firm. Of his other child Mary, little is recorded beyond her marriage to Josiah Gaunt, a Leek silk manufacturer.

Henry Davenport was born in 1800. Nothing is known of his early life and schooling, but in 1817 his father writing from Longport on 7 July clearly regards him as a part of the firm:

> Dear Henry,
>
> I have sent instructions to James Sherwin to proceed immediately to St Petersburg, and if you desire to go with him lose no time in getting down to Hambro' . . .
>
> You had expressed a wish once to accompany some officer to this same place—is my reason for making you this offer—Mr Sherwin you will find with Jos'h Davenport at Grosse Johannes Strasse No 59 in Hamburg—the route you take I leave to your Judgment . . . (*Foxley*, 35)

Here is documentary evidence of the existence of a Hamburg warehouse in 1817 at the address given. (By 1840 the warehouse address was 4 Grosse-Johannes Strasse.) It is not known at what date this connection was established. But for the war, one might have surmised a long-standing connection, for Sleigh records a Uriah Davenport and a branch of the family as resident in Hamburg in the early eighteenth century. There were certainly 'cousins' and other relatives in charge of the Hamburg warehouse and showrooms for many years after 1817.

Henry Davenport presumably made the journey to Hamburg and St Petersburg. There is no doubt from the correspondence that he was taking a full and active part in the concern of John & James Davenport by 1822. He then wrote to his father (who seems to have settled temporarily in London at Salisbury Square) about 'China clay, I will not part with an ounce more untill (sic) I know where the next is to come from, we have got the last up from Runcorn, it will not answer to have to buy at £6 perhaps after selling at £4 10s . . .' (*Foxley*, 11). Again on 28 May 1822 he reports on various matters to his father:

> Fynney . . . left early next morning for L'pool, thus putting an end to my journey thither. I will have him up again before long for I cannot fix any prices *there*, I shall not have any support. I think an Agency will do as well in L'pool as a Co-partnership; it would not answer with everyone but I am sure he will act in every respect as if the concern was his own . . .
>
> You may be on the lookout for a bookkeeper, the animal we have here will have notice to leave in a few days, you would not bear him a week, he is a double Marmot, he sleeps both winter and summer . . .
>
> I am D'r Father,
> Y'r dutiful Son,
> H'y Davenport. (*Foxley*, 13)

It seems likely that John Davenport left the day to day management of the Longport works very much in Henry's hands from this time forward. In London he would be partly occupied with the business of the new London showroom situated at 82 Fleet Street which had been leased in 1818. (A picture of the premises drawn by G. James Findlay c 1845 is shown as Pl 25b in Bevis Hillier's book on the Turners.)

The *Foxley Papers* reveal the range of Henry's managerial activities and enlarge our understanding of the nature of the firm's development. In 1823 he visited the Liverpool warehouse and consulted with the manager Mountford Fynney as to the price of a lease on a new warehouse. 'As regards the capital necessary for this concern, Fynney thinks that from thirty to forty thousand pounds will be quite ample . . .' (*Foxley*, 16, dated 21 Aug 1823). The Liverpool warehouse was eventually sited at 36 Canning Place. In 1825 on the instructions of his father he visited an agent called Close in Cornwall concerning the clay supplies and the state of the mines at Gonnomaris and Hensbarrow. 'What you go for is to prevent anyone from getting clay from *Close but ourselves*' (*Foxley*, 36). Such was the instruction from John Davenport. Henry's report back upon his visit did not please his father who wrote:

> . . . I am led to think you are not well satisfied with yourself on the subject of your Cornish journey for nothing which I have written ought to have drawn forth the testy observations contained in it [Henry's report] . . . I have often had to complain of a lack of correspondence but I would rather be without it, than to receive such as that now before me, which I think is neither respectful towards me nor creditable to yourself as it displays a great want of temper . . . while I have anything to do with the concern I will not be debarred from making any observations which I think proper to make on the conduct of it in whose hands soever it be placed . . . (*Foxley*, 37).

If Henry and his younger brother felt their father's disapprobation from time to time, it was as nothing to the invective reserved for the Pontignys. Henry Pontigny entered the concern in 1820 at the London showroom and his son Victor joined him in 1823. In May 1825 Henry Pontigny became a partner in the business as the following circular letter to clients indicates.

> Longport Pottery and Glass Works,
> Staffordshire. 14th April 1825.
>
> Sir,
>
> I beg to inform you that from the time of the decease of my late Copartner Mr James Davenport, I have taken into Copartnership my son Henry Davenport, who has had for some time the Direction of the Manufactories in Staffordshire, Mr Mountford Fynney, who for many years has managed our Concerns at Liverpool, and Mr Henry Pontigny with whom I have been long connected in London.
>
> From the 1st of May next, the Business will be conducted under the following Firms.
>
> At Longport. . John Davenport, Son & Co.
> At Liverpool. . Davenports, Fynney & Co.
> in London. . . . Davenports, Pontigny & Co . . .
>
> I am very respectfully,
> Sir,
> Your obliged humble Serv't.
> J'n Davenport. (*Foxley*, 29)

Pontigny's share in the concern was an eighth. Not mentioned in the circular is the sleeping partner Thomas Kinnersley who had a quarter share. At the end of 1825, Kinnersley was in financial difficulties. John Davenport came to his aid. In two letters to Henry (*Foxley*, 40 and 41, the first dated 22 December 1825, the second undated but written very shortly afterwards) John Davenport reveals the tremendously secure financial position of the concern. 'A guarantee would be found in a day for 200,000 if it was required—my name would stand good for 40-50,000, I think almost anywhere.' In the second letter he adds: 'I have at length succeeded for Kinnersley, the Bank of England will lend him 80,000 and I have reason to believe on our security—that is me accepting or indorsing his Bills' [of Exchange].

To return to Henry Pontigny; he clearly was a man of Gallic *élan* and enthusiasm, his letters make delightful reading. Shortly after becoming a partner he wrote an important letter to Henry Davenport which epitomises the rather haphazard and unsystematic business methods of the period, and yet reveals his own infectious delight at outwitting the opposition. From London dated 26 Oct 1825, he writes:

> Dear Henry,
>
> Old Spode is melted. He has published a New List, which I shall get as soon as I can. We must filigree him again to punish him for plaguing us so much. I wrote you some time back I had got hold of one of his Netherlands Customers. I had yesterday one of his Paris folks and am going to sell him Ewers, Basins, Chambers, Soap & Brush Boxes in China, the value and price of which I am sure I am quite ignorant of. I presume you make or can make in China all the Patterns of Ironstone, but *entre nous* I wish you would let me into the secret of the difference of value between the same articles in Ironstone & China—Ironstone is not admitted in France, China is, at the duty of 345 francs for every 210 lbs weight. You might perhaps well *rougir* yourself about your price of *Rougepots*. Why not make a doz or two to ascertain price. It never could be 2/6—I shall get them from Rose at half the price.
>
> I am afraid the Stone Closetpans even at 6/- with the Tablets will not do. If they are not worth more than Handbasons 6s, surely 36/- per

doz is too much.—Herbert Minton does not charge the Blueprinted Earthenware more than 2/- ea(ch) to Hawkings—and if he be right in his Calculations the Stone should not cost more than 4/- or 4/6 and with the Tablet 5/- . . .

Arroyave is going to be married and will have One of your New Ironstone Table sets.—I am sorry to say that every body prefers Hicks & Cos' No 9 to any of ours. (*Foxley*, 38)

This enthusiasm was short-lived. Within a twelvemonth Pontigny's tone had changed considerably. In a long letter dated 22 April 1826 (unfortunately torn in parts) he complains—amongst other things:

Your father has treated me very ill. I can bear [tear] as most men, but there is so much malignity [tear] Behaviour, that I cannot, will not indeed put [tear] He has insulted, vilified me openly; his turning me out of the House, has been the common talk of all the neighbourhood & of all the Establishment. If therefore he does not retrace *all* his steps I will not remain in the Concern, and the Sooner I go out of it, the Better; as really my health & spirits demand some immediate relaxation.

I have for nearly six years now, been a complete slave to this Concern, and if I am not treated by the Head of it with Common Courtesy, I will not continue in it an hour . . .

This my dear Henry is the State of Affairs. And as I said before unless your father will retrace *all* his steps, I must bid you farewell . . . (*Foxley*, 43).

Three weeks later he again writes forcefully:

Mr Fynney would have given me much less trouble about Brough had he informed me exactly when he meant to leave Longport—But I suppose in the *True Davenport Style*, he never read the play of *Know Your Own Mind* . . .

I have explained what I want about prices, and if you or Mr D— will not understand me, I cannot help it. It is ridiculous to say that we must sell for what we can get. We must have a price arranged for the times and carry on trade with some system as I have no traveller I can trust to sell at different lists, and indeed it is utterly impossible to attempt . . .

Times are bad, very bad, but yet we could easily go thro, them, were we, as we should [be] unanimous in furthering the Interest of the Concern. Mr D— has broken all the ties which attached me to it, and as I only wish to get out of it altogether, I feel neither inclination nor duty to make me a slave to this business when I am so ill repaid for all my anxiety . . . (*Foxley*, 44).

It is worth remarking how this highly successful firm seemed to manage their affairs so ill. But these were early days, industrially speaking. There was no trained managerial class, no Colleges of Commerce, none of the aids to commercial practice with which we are so familiar. There was a man with a quill pen and, if he was lucky, a few subordinates who could read and write. It is small wonder that letters were lost or not answered, wrong prices quoted and debts and bills overlooked. The marvel is that men like John Davenport prospered so exceedingly when the logistics which supported their operations were so frail. John Davenport was aware of this weakness. He admonished Henry for his carelessness in composing a letter for Rostock:

. . . the whole letter seems to have been written in great haste without considering that it would take a long time to get an explanation of anything [that] was not understood. The care with which correspondence should be conducted, should be proportionate to the distance and means of ready communication. It might have done to send to Whitehaven or Hull but is rather too short and inexplicit for the Baltic, in winter too . . . (*Foxley*, 42, dated 14 January 1826.)

Whatever the rights and wrongs of the Pontigny affair, the partnership was too stormy to last. On 19 June 1827, a Memorandum of Agreement was signed between Henry Davenport and Henry Pontigny by which Davenport purchased all Pontigny's interests in the concerns for £8,500. The following day a notice of the dissolution of their partnerships appeared in the *London Gazette* (20 June 1827, p 2,650).

The withdrawal of Pontigny may have been a cause of dispute between John Davenport and his sons, for towards the end of the same year he wrote an extraordinary letter to Henry. It is dated 11 Nov 1827 and has apparently no heading and no signature:

As H.D. has not thought it needful or proper to give his brother W.D. any employment at Longport J.D. wishes to know H.D.'s views &

wishes respecting him—and as to the part he is expected to take, or will take in the Concerns. . . . That he has not been more closely employed there [Longport] has been very unsatisfactory to J.D.—and detrimental to himself—but J.D. has always had great objections to forcing any thing so as to create disquiets— . . . H.D. & W.D. are requested to consult on these affairs and present some plan on which they are agreeable to act with proper effect in supporting the different concerns, and if needful of extending them & making them sufficiently profitable—and so as to require no further interference or direction from their Father who desires to retire from all Business and will short likely (*sic*) leave this part of the Country entirely—

J.D. prefers this being done by H.D. & W.D. rather than to lay down any plan himself which might not be approved & consequently not acted upon. (*Foxley*, 47.)

Presumably Henry's reply satisfied him, or the possible departure from the concern of Thomas Kinnersley left him no time for further recriminations, for on 27 December he wrote an affable letter discussing the possible distribution of shares if Kinnersley did withdraw and ends his letter skittishly with a personal note presumably relating to his daughter, 'Mrs Bent', who has returned to her husband:

. . . All flirtations—but carried further than English customs yet allow—we are however progressing in this, as in many other relations of society towards the demoralizing customs of our continental neighbours.

I am, with love to you all . . . (*Foxley*, 48.)

The outcome of the discussions concerning Kinnersley was that he was bought out at a cost of £17,000 early in 1828. There was clearly further tension over this move and over the general management of the concern, for John Davenport, writing to Henry on 12 January 1828, reminds him: 'You have promised to make the next five years better than the last, and £4,000 added to your income would be worth a great deal of Shooting and Coursing . . .' (*Foxley*, 51.)

As an incidental he adds that according to the Stock Books the value of all the china on 16 January 1828, 'amounts to £7,047 16s. $2\frac{1}{2}$d'. Typically he also notes that there is an accounting error, as no note has been taken of discounts.

As might be anticipated, the Pontigny affair was not yet over. John Davenport was being difficult about the payment of Pontigny's one-eighth share, valued at about £8,500. In a tone of pained resignation Henry Pontigny wrote to Henry Davenport yet again:

. . . I have not succeeded to come to a settlement with your father. He has been very industriously employed to find some mistake in the London Account, which he has not succeeded in. At last on Monday he did fairly inform me he would not settle the account, nor pay me at present any more money, upon which I made my arrangements to go to the Continent . . .

I expect to spend next winter either in Nice and Piedmont or in Spain, in either case I might sell a few mugs for you. I proposed it to your father who seemed not to care much about it . . .

In reviewing past events I cannot charge myself with any impropriety in respect of your father. Poor as I am, I feel much happier in my present state of independence than I should with any prospect of Fortune as his Partner. I have now but a few years to live: and these I hope I shall spend quietly and without any of these feverish feelings, which you know by experience, as well as I do . . . (*Foxley*, 54, dated 31 May 1828.)

Ultimately, Pontigny must have been paid in full. But with the departure of the father, the son Victor became the object of John Davenport's wrath. On 7 January 1831, he enquired of Henry:

. . . But as to London I must ask you what is to be done with the management of this concern? I cannot undertake it and as to Victor Pontigny he is, if possible, more trifling and addling than even was his father—he does really nothing, yet is always busy . . . (*Foxley*, 59)

He adds, 'Our affairs don't seem in good trim anywhere.' This latter statement is rather surprising since in 1830 the concern had received a commission to produce a dessert service for William IV (an important matter dealt with fully on pp 78-84). Moreover, only nine months earlier (on 22 April 1830) Davenport had written to his son William, 'Henry & I both think that now our China is so fine we ought to have some sort of standing at the West End, some one to show it and sell it, if not a concern wholly our own . . .' (*Foxley*, 76). But then, as we have already noted,

John Davenport was nothing if not mercurial in his moods. By this date, 1830, he had reached the age of sixty-five, and as sometimes happens in men of this age, he became stubborn, self-righteous and unsympathetic to the ideas and opinions of his juniors in age and experience. He became, as Reginald Haggar so aptly put it, 'an old curmudgeon'.

It was not merely Victor Pontigny who incurred his abuse. When Henry Davenport queried a request for the ledgers and detailed accounts for 1827 and 1828 to be sent to London he received the full force of his father's displeasure:

Of old it was so, a man might do as he would with his own, but times are changed it seems . . . You have not it appears understood me. I had told you some time ago how I had then disposed of my property & the reasons for so doing—I now purpose a change in the direction, and to enable me to deal justly, as I may think, though others may 'kick' & think differently, I required the account & valuations mentioned to you—

It would afford me sincere pleasure to be persuaded that no dissensions would arise after I am gone but present appearances rather lead me to apprehend it may be otherwise and I wish therefore to make my arrangement in a way to prevent disputes hereafter . . . I will mention to you one little fact which has struck me lately, not one of my family have given me the least hint of what has happened at Westwood by the birth of a Grandson—I shall make no comments only that it interests me much as to think it worth noting.

I agree with you that profits in trade are only made by savings—but a man may for want of a general superintendance lose or waste, or rather have lost & wasted, at one place more than he saves at another—and I feel this to be a fact in particular as regards London—where a fellow that did us a great harm & frustrated our business, has been allowed to swallow near Ten Thousand pounds of our money . . . The trade here [London] I think may be mended, but not without a better direction—Victor like his father, will never get a shilling in the mug trade—' (*Foxley*, 62, from London dated 26 January 1831.)

Davenport ends with the passage already quoted about his possible return to residence at Westwood.

Clearly, something was amiss both with the management of the concern, and with the personal relationships of its proprietors and their senior employees. Before the year (1831) was out John Davenport had made a strong attempt to get rid of Victor Pontigny. Writing to William from London on 21 March he says:

. . . It would be ridiculous to leave Victor Pontigny at the head of our affairs [in London], indeed he is of little use whatever to us, and I presume his services must be dispensed with for a cashkeeper, he is not worth his salary—he continues as shuffling & trifling as ever, and I can't improve him—but the best thing would be to give up the concern altogether. (*Foxley*, 18)

A little later he returns to the theme in a further letter from London, this time to Henry, dated 21 Sept 1831:

. . . I wish to know if you said anything to Victor about leaving, he must really go—He serves only for an authority for every thing being neglected, & for shuffling of every kind whatsoever. He will be as unfit for a Coadjutor with Jos. D. as he has been with Master William—he is the completest trifler in existence. (*Foxley*, 63)

The following day he again presses the point of Victor's incompetence:

. . . He seems much annoyed, says he never has been tried, *or left to himself* or he could do wonders—but he will never astonish anyone in the Mug Trade, whatever he may do in the Orchestra or quizzing room—but he is a trifler and a shuffler & not worth so much time . . . (*Foxley*, 64, dated 22 September 1831.)

Presumably Henry Davenport was not to be bullied by his father on these matters and Victor was still in office in 1835 and echoing his father's complaints of ten years earlier when he writes: 'Mr D. is using me very strangely. He has now taken it into his head that I "do nothing".' (*Foxley*, 74, dated 13 August 1835.) To prove his value he submitted the trade figures quoted on p 19 (see also page 64).

It is possible that Victor Pontigny owed his continued employment after 1831 to the absorption of John Davenport in political affairs. This was the period of the struggle for the passing of the Reform Bill. Amongst the provisions of the Bill was a plan to redistribute seats in the House of Commons. Somewhat ironically, in view of subsequent events, John Davenport noted, 'I see you [at Stoke] are going to petition the House of Lords for two members, it will be of no use, but of course it may be tried . . .' (*Foxley*, 65, dated 27 September 1831.) In the event it was tried and was successful. The story of this first Parliamentary election in Stoke is detailed in Ward (pp 62-3) and an additional and longer account is contained in Reginald Haggar's book on *The Masons of Lane Delph* (pp 37-41).

John Davenport stood as a candidate along with Josiah Wedgwood, a fellow Tory; the Radical George Miles Mason was also in the lists as was Richard Edensor Heathcote of Longton Hall, of whom John Davenport had written, 'It will be our business however to support any other candidate in opposition to him—if only from personal motives—and this he ought to know & feel' (*Foxley*, 67, London, 3 Oct 1831). This was written before he himself became a candidate. In his election address a copy of which is preserved at Hanley Museum, Davenport claims to have completed a canvass which 'place it beyond a doubt' that he will be elected. There is a typical Davenport flourish as he declares:

> I have to complain, that in the outset of this contest, my opponents charged me with Bigotry in Religion, and in Politics and as being opposed to the Education of the People. But I have been gratified to find how little these malignant aspersions have been believed; from men of all persuasions in Religion, and from men differing in some degree in Politics, I have received unqualified support.

After a long justification of his attitude to Church Reform ('I am no Bigot') he professes his support of the reform of Parliament, adds a paragraph on the abolition of Slavery ('we can all have but one end in view . . . *the comfort and happiness of the Slave*.'), a paragraph on general trade and working conditions and ends with a pledge to devote himself entirely to the service of his constituents. The manifesto, one might assume of a moderate and sincere reformer. That is not, however, the light in which he was seen by many people. John Henry Clive (1781-1853), a master-potter, engraver, colliery proprietor and inventor wrote a skit on the election shortly after polling day in December 1832. This *Chronicle* was reproduced by Percy W. L. Adams in his biography of Clive. The *Chronicle* runs to six chapters of 155 verses in a mock-Biblical fashion. The verse is excruciating, but its spirit serves to illustrate the feelings current towards Davenport:

> Do I not know that I am not liked in the land of my birth, but they are a people given to filthy lucre. I will open the store houses of my wealth. I will unlock my treasures unto them and they will look upon my face as upon the face of an angel.

It is not surprising to find on reading the more prosaic accounts of the election that 'whilst Mr Davenport was addressing the Electors, missiles were profusely thrown into the hustings, which inflicted some severe contusions on several gentlemen.' The windows of Davenport's committee rooms were smashed and houses of his supporters attacked. Mason asserted that 'one twelfth part of the voters may be bought by one rich man'. There seems little doubt that John Davenport's *Canvass* must have cost him a great deal in bribes. Unfortunately, the *Foxley* papers appear to have no record of this activity. Polling took place on 11 and 12 December 1832 at Burslem, Hanley, Stoke and Lane End. Davenport and Wedgwood were elected (the full details of the poll are given in both Ward and Haggar). John Davenport, at the age of sixty-seven, was a Member of Parliament.

His new responsibilities did not distract his attention from business. The stream of letters from London to Henry and William continued. It is impossible to accept the customary statement that John Davenport retired from business in 1830. Day-to-day management at Longport had been in Henry Davenport's hands certainly as early as 1825 and possibly from 1822. By 1826 John was established semi-permanently in London, but as the fine letter (*Foxley*, 73) quoted on p 52 indicates, his interest in the workings of the firm was still intense. On the other hand, the continued presence of Victor Pontigny argues that, after the re-arrangements following the withdrawal of Henry Pontigny and Kinnersley, it was Henry Davenport who now wielded the power of hiring and firing. But this is all speculation. We are on sure ground in recording that John Davenport retained his Parliamentary seat in the election of 6 January 1835. In 1837 (on the death of William IV) Ward notes, 'Mr Davenport, however, was reluctant to be put again in nomination, on account of his age and infirmities, but was prevailed upon to comply with the wishes of his friends, to nominate and re-elect him without any personal trouble or expense.' Again, apparently, there were 'disgraceful scenes' but Davenport was duly elected, along with his fellow-Conservative, William Taylor Copeland who had recently acquired the Spode factory.

Miller notes that John Davenport retired from all business and settled down at Westwood in 1838. This seems a reasonable assumption for he did not contest the 1841 election.

If politics had partly preoccupied John Davenport after 1832, there is no indication that the concern suffered in any way. Henry Davenport was responsible for the management at Longport and there is evidence (see p 111) that the title of the firm changed from John Davenport, Son & Co as it had been in 1825, to Henry & William Davenport & Co. There is documentary confirmation of this and evidence of further expansion in a set of *Articles of Agreement* dated 11 December 1834 preserved in the Hanley Museum records. The articles give details of the purchase by Henry Davenport of premises, namely 'potworks, erections and buildings heretofore erected and built by the said Hugh Henshall . . . adjoining up to certain other potworks and Buildings lately purchased by the said Hugh Henshall Williamson and together forming one set of potworks lately in the holding of Robert Williamson and Company and now of Henry & William Davenport & Company . . .'

The purchase price is given as £2,500 for completion on 1 May 1835. The addition of the Williamson works to the Newport and Longport factories and the glass works gave the Davenports control over the largest factory then operating in Staffordshire.

Henry Davenport had very little time in which to enjoy the ownership of his new factory. His addiction to hunting—he was MFH at Baddeley Edge—proved fatal. He 'met with his death by a fall from his horse' on 13 November 1835. A memorial tablet is to be found in St Paul's Church, Dale Hall, Burslem. From the evidence of the *Foxley* papers, Henry seems a likeable character. He was not as arrogant as his father, and he lacked his drive and ruthlessness. His life was easier than John Davenport's had been, he was born into comparative affluence, and though he may have been lazy and self-indulgent, he must have been a more congenial man to work for than his father.

With the death of Henry and the virtual retirement of John Davenport, an era was at an end. The concern passed into the hands of William Davenport. However, the *Foxley* papers, of which the latest dated (coincidentally) is from 1835, are worth a further examination for the light they throw upon the foreign trade of Davenports and the pertinacity with which John Davenport sought to expand overseas connections.

A note has already been made of the journey of Henry Davenport to St Petersburg in 1817 and of the establishment in Hamburg. In 1822 John Davenport received a long letter dated 6 July from Samuel Hopkins his agent in Messina. Hopkins had been there for eighteen years and wrote seeking a post in England. He had acted as Davenport's agent for the previous four years (1818-22). This fits in well with the known desire for export expansion once the Napoleonic wars had ended (*Foxley*, 14). The following year, 1823, James Davenport (junior) wrote to John Davenport on 3 September thanking him for his advice on a projected establishment at Brussels. He maintains that Brussels is preferable to Rotterdam. It seems possible that he settled there for a brief period, though there is no further record of this in the documents other than two letters of the same year, one from Henry Pontigny to John Davenport is dated 1 November 1823, in which he recommends 'a steady clever young man of 25 or 26 years of age' as a partner to James Davenport in Brussels. He adds: 'His father is a man of Property (and "a very particular friend of mine") and would advance £1,500 to £2,000 sterling to put him in business . . . he will make a very active traveller and the knowledge of languages will be very necessary for that Department.' He ends with a typical Pontigny phrase, 'of earthenware he knows nothing'. (*Foxley*, 19). A further letter from John Davenport to William, who was staying in Nantes dated 5 November 1823, confirms the intention that James Davenport 'is going to fix himself in Brussels'. He adds that he is:

> . . . in hopes we shall have some trade to Spain, indeed orders for the North part are coming in—as to France & her foolish prohibitory system, for the present I have no hopes, yet I trust the

lesson given to her in the Netherlands will have some effect—Trade every where ought to be without restrictions . . . (*Foxley*, 75).

It seems possible that some form of agency was established in Brussels, but unlikely that it continued for any length of time as James Davenport (junior) was in charge of the Hamburg establishment (possibly after the 1825 re-organisation) with his brothers Uriah and Joseph.

There is a gap in the documents from 1823 to 1828 as far as foreign trade is concerned, with the exception of some matters relating to Hamburg. But that does not mean that Davenport wares were not finding markets abroad. An auctioneer's advertisement in the Canadian paper the *Novascotian* on 6 December 1827 offered amongst the household furnishings, 'a dinner set, DAVENPORT WARE, 274 pieces' (E. Collard, p 243). Presumably, these wares had been exported some time previously. As Mrs Collard comments, 'Davenport became a household word' throughout North America.

In 1828 we find John Davenport exploring even further afield. On 12 January he asks Henry:

. . . to pay more attention to the Rio orders—to have them done in the very best manner that we may establish a regular trade, even a monopoly of the trade to that place—It is far preferable to any round Cape Horn or to Mexico . . . (*Foxley*, 51).

He also comments that a shipping agent in Liverpool has failed to pay for consignments of wares sent to Lima. A fortnight later, 26 January 1828, he again instructs Henry:

Fynney must look for some one to go to the US:—he can spare Everard for a twelve month—and our surplus stock would sell at Auction there better than in London . . . also as to Pontigny going to Spain—I don't think it would do much good for us . . . (*Foxley*, 53).

In 1830 John Davenport noted to William that some goods of theirs had once been sent by an agent 'from Buenos Aires to Valparaiso where they brought nothing, but we made him account for them—as being sent without our orders' (*Foxley*, 76). In 1831 Davenport again took up the subject of the North American market, presumably Fynney had not found anyone to go out there for he writes to Henry:

. . . What we have first to ascertain is the actual value of a piece of our Wares in the United States for unless a profit can be made we should not attempt to take up that trade—But I must remark that the quickness of returns compared with those from S America & the E Indies would make less capital necessary . . . (*Foxley*, 61, dated 22 January 1831.)

Some weeks later John Davenport offered, as was his wont, some words of general advice to William:

. . . a foreign trade can never be conducted with success unless the most minute and continual attention is paid to what is going on in the Sales, & in the collection of the monies at the periods when they become due . . . (*Foxley*, 81, dated 21 Mar 1831.)

By 1836 the firm had found a reliable agent in North America for Davenport wares were being specially marked with the name of *Henderson & Gaines, Importers, 45 Canal St., New Orleans* (see pp 56-7). If we add to these quoted outlets, the making of special wares for regiments in India, and a steady stream of goods sent to Hamburg, there is no doubt of the importance to the prosperity of the concern of its export trade. Indeed, John Davenport in a fit of depression in July 1832 when cholera was confirmed in London wrote:

. . . foreign powers will interdict all commerce with our shores now they are infected, and what that may lead to, God Knows—would not it be wise to hoard a few Guineas . . . if the Hamburg house fails us we shall be deeply injured . . . (*Foxley*, 68, dated 14 July 1832).

As the Hamburg house was given a net cash value at this date of £3,560, Davenport's alarm may have had some validity.

A fitting final word on foreign trade may be provided by Victor Pontigny. Stung by John Davenport's accusation that he 'never gets 1/- for this concern', he sent to Henry a balance sheet of exports for the half-year ending 30 June 1835:

. . . Export to Spain	856.15.8
to Italy	310.13.10
	1,166.19.6
to Sundries	1,191.11.8
	£2,358.11.2

> London profit & above Port Invoices—say 15 pc (full) £353.15.0 *which is £707.10.0 profit p[er] annum* (*Foxley*, 74).

The Years of Success (c 1835-1869) William Davenport & Co

Upon the death of Henry Davenport, the business passed into the hands of his younger brother, and until his death in 1869, the firm was styled William Davenport & Co. As the *Foxley* papers contain no letters after 1835 there is no guidance as to the part played by John Davenport. If we assume that he retired from *all* business in 1838, there is some justification for thinking that once the disturbance created by Henry's death had been settled, he paid little further attention to the pottery business. His relationship with William was ambivalent, to say the least. He was always less cordial with him than with Henry, and at times he seemed positively antagonistic. On 12 January 1828, John Davenport writing to Henry observes:

> Why should not Will go down to take his [Fynney's] place for a time while he Recruits? It is high time that young man should make himself of some real value in our concerns, at his Age I had been more than two years in Business, I got through it without any direction & with very little assistance—let him be put on his mettle somewhat & if he breaks down, turn him out of the Stud—but I have better hopes of him . . . (*Foxley*, 51).

Again in an undated letter of 1831, John enquires:

> . . . What am I to do with Will. He is of no use to me here—at least but little—He has had new clothes—the lad is very attentive and obliging . . . (*Foxley*, 57).

'The lad' was twenty-six years old at the time! Later in the same year, at a time when he was recovering from illness and expressed annoyance, 'at being tied like a Bear to the Stake here when I ought to be enjoying a quiet retirement and preparing myself for another and I trust a better world' (*Foxley*, 122, dated 17 September 1831), John Davenport complains of 'the scrawl sent me by W. D. & which I returned to him in town with a request to have it completed in a better manner' (*Foxley*, 63, dated 21 Sept 1831). The following day he wrote, 'I think you noticed to Master William what I said about his first and last letter since he left London, and you may add to it that I shall care as little about him as he cares about me . . .' (*Foxley*, 64).

This then was the man in whose hands the future of the firm rested after 1835. In view of his father's opinion of him it is perhaps surprising that the concern prospered so greatly under his guidance. At this date William Davenport had been married for three years to Marianne the daughter of the much-esteemed John Wood of Brownhills. Their first child Henry was born in 1840 and it was he who eventually inherited the business on his father's death in 1869. William and Marianne Davenport had eight further children—all girls. The first five—their names have a fine Victorian ring about them—Mary, Emily Anne, Constance Clementina, Agnes and Alice Jessie were all successfully matched in marriage in due course. But the provision of eight marriage settlements must have been too much for even the wealthiest of master-potters, and the three youngest, Diane Elizabeth, Sarah Ellen and Marianne Henrietta remained spinsters.

The enterprise which William Davenport now controlled was a very substantial one. In addition to the original Unicorn Bank and the glass works were the Newport Works and the recently-acquired factory of Williamson & Co. Alexander Brongniart in his *Traité des Arts Ceramiques* (Vol II, 1836, p 453, quoted in J. C. Wedgwood) notes that some 1,400 workpeople were employed by the company. He further estimated that the value of china and earthenware produced annually was in the region of £100,000. If this is anywhere nearly accurate—and we have no other evidence—it represents an enormous number of pots. If one considers that 'One hogshead containing one dinner set of light blue printed earthenware, gilt knobs and handles for twenty-four persons' in all

220 pieces, was priced in 1848 for export to India at £16 less 10 per cent discount, the sheer number of pots Brogniart's estimate involves is staggering.

William Davenport was to add one further factory to his holdings. Some time in the early 1840s, the premises originally erected in 1775 by Edward Bourne were purchased. Thus when Ward wrote in 1843—he was speaking in terms of three potbanks in Longport and a glass works as well as an earthenware factory at Newport—'the aggregate of their businesses indeed is of a very considerable magnitude, and gives employment to upwards of fifteen hundred hands.'

For this period of the firm's history there is very little original documentary material. We know from the general histories of the period such as those of Harold Owen, Dr J. H. Thomas and W. H. Warburton that the 1830s and 1840s in particular were periods of considerable labour unrest and deplorable working conditions in many of the Staffordshire potbanks. The evils of 'good from oven', the allowance system, annual hiring and truck payments are beyond the scope of this work, as are the great strikes of 1834 and 1836. It would be pleasant to record that in these times the Davenports were model employers. Unfortunately, this is not the case. The evidence we have comes from C. Shaw (An Old Potter) writing of his childhood experiences in *When I was a child*. This remarkable book is worthy of study by all who give more than a passing thought to the men, women and children who produced the pots which adorn the collector's cabinet. Shaw writes with great feeling of the early 1840s when as a child he worked first as a mould-runner, then at the age of eight as a handle-maker. He writes at length of the conditions under which he toiled with a farthing candle for illumination in the ill-lit and fetid atmosphere of the basement of a large factory of externally-imposing aspect. The flavour of the original is almost impossible to recreate, and too lengthy to quote in detail, but when he writes of the brutality of the young man for whom he worked, and of the drunkenness and all-night orgies ('the night was a revel of drink, lust and beastliness') and when he recalls that as a child of nine he worked for seventy to eighty hours a week, getting home at nine or ten o'clock at night having left between four and five in the morning, and for this he received one and sixpence or two shillings a week, it is not difficult to agree that 'the evils of this Pottery works were perhaps the result of the cold, aristocratic attitude of this employer towards his own business.'

Was 'this employer' John Davenport? The evidence is not conclusive for Shaw would 'not indicate where this bank was as some persons yet living may be pained by identification . . . with such memories'. He adds that 'no one is now living who was responsible in any way for the things of which I write'.

It has generally been assumed that this dreadful example of the more savage and inhuman aspects of the Industrial Revolution was one of the Davenport potteries. Shaw came from Tunstall; his father, as we shall see, was a Davenport employee; he writes of his employer 'away in his country mansion' and of his being a 'county magistrate'. Even more pointedly he writes of himself being transferred 'to work at the lower bank, where chinaware was manufactured [where] . . . there was no trace of the drunken rowdyism which prevailed at the higher works'. The use of lower and higher, are surely significant for, as Scarrett reminds us, two of the Davenport manufactories at Tunstall/Longport were the Bottom-bridge Bank and the Top-bridge Bank. There really seems to be no other set of works and employers in 1840-2 who fit the descriptions given. However, perhaps deliberately, Shaw gives no hint that he and his father ever worked in the same place; he writes of the men at the old china bank who were really artists; 'they modelled specially beautiful figures in Parian'. Now unless they never marked their pieces, Davenports do not appear to have made parian ware. (Moreover, 1842 is a suspiciously early date for this material. See p 106). Shaw's information concerning his employers is also often confusing (pp 51 and 75), though he draws a vivid picture of 'a later employer' (presumably William Davenport) who:

> . . . very occasionally came through the shop with a tall silk hat on, and a swallow-tailed coat and shining boots. His habit was never to stop a moment, but to look up and forward, over the heads of the workpeople, with his hands under his coat tails, which tails were incessantly tossed, looking as if he had come on parade to show the awful or sublime contrast between his special humanity and that of the drudging humanity

around him . . . This swallow-tailed coat 'master' . . . some years before was a warehouseman . . . (*Shaw*, p 75).

This seems to be an authentic description of William Davenport who had indeed served in the warehouse at both Longport and London when his father sought to train him.

There is no ambiguity at all about the description Shaw gives of the treatment his father received from William Davenport. He writes:

My maternal grandfather [James Mawdesley, Davenport's manager c 1815] was honoured by his employer, while my father was ruined by the same employer's son. This was done with such calculated deliberation and with such force of animus that, as I shall show, it gave me residence in Chell, where I began to have experience of the new Poor Law . . . My father, as I have stated, was 'a painter and gilder'. He worked at Davenport's. A new manager there introduced new methods of conducting the business. For one thing he introduced female labour in a department which had hitherto belonged almost exclusively to the men. This new competition was resisted, partly as an innovation and partly because of the serious reduction in wages it involved.

The men resented and resisted the change. They struck work with the winter before them, and with no organisation on which to depend for assistance. They had no resources whatever . . .

I suppose my father must have been a sort of ringleader in this strike, for many years after, I saw a letter from his brother-in-law, who was one of the managers of the works, to say that, if he did not give up his support of the strike, Mr D. had told him he would ruin him, and force him and his family into the workhouse. This bitter prophecy became bitterly true. Such intimidation in those days could be easily carried out by employers . . . It appears that my father would not be 'intimidated', nor would he desist in his efforts to maintain the strike. So we were indeed driven into the workhouse. I have sometimes wondered whether a direct Nemesis was sent to balance this sorry, reckless piece of vengeance. It would be easy to unfold a harrowing tale of what followed this man's wild revenge in his family history. In this matter, to attempt to trace cause and effect would be inexpressible presumption, but, at the same time, coincidences arrest attention . . .

Shaw's father eventually obtained another job and the family left the dreaded workhouse. Shaw is naturally a very biased witness. As a Methodist minister, he abhorred the effects of drink, and his picture of the potbank may well be tinged by a retrospective desire to use the incidents he relates as propaganda for total abstinence. But, there is no denying the treatment meted out to his father by William Davenport. All the impressions that have been formed of William indicate a cold and pseudo-aristocratic hauteur, a disregard for his workpeople and a concentration on what Shaw calls the 'cash-nexus'.

One interesting side-light of Shaw's account is his statement that 'the year that man drove my father to the workhouse, I have since learned, he bought an estate for about £200,000. Yet trade was so bad he had to reduce the wages of his painters and gilders' (Shaw, p 118). The estate referred to would be the Maer estate bought from the Wedgwoods in 1843—though the price seems inordinately high. Shaw adds, 'I will not say how Nemesis has worked since, but that estate belongs to no descendant of his today' (see below p 31).

It is perhaps worth emphasising that the 'princely fortunes' made by the Davenports were not simply the profits of the pottery and glass businesses. They had extensive holdings of land, of canal shares and property in and around Leek and Stoke, as well as interests in coal mines, railways and Government stock. Their investments were spread very widely.

It is possible that John Davenport never even heard of the strike of 1842. At this stage he had retired to Westwood and William was fully in charge of the firm. In his eightieth year on 24 March 1845 the old man made his will. In true Davenport style, he altered it without the witnesses having been aware of the alterations, and subsequently he added two Codicils. One on 26 January 1847 is in his own hand which is still firm and clearly legible, and a second on 18 March 1848 which is merely signed rather shakily by Davenport and is the more important. In his original will he had left sums of money to his daughter Elizabeth Bent and his 'faithful servant Margaret Martin' and 'all the residue of my personal estate and effects . . . to my said son John absolutely . . . And I give devise and appoint unto my said son John his heirs and assigns all my real estate whatsoever . . .' John was also appointed Executor.

The second codicil to the will protected the position of William, for in considerable detail certain properties and lands connected with the business were specified which were bequeathed to William:

> . . . I give and devise all those my Earthenware Manufactory, Glass Works, Dwelling houses and other erections, Land and premises with the appurtenances situate at Longport . . . in the occupation of William Davenport & Co . . . and also a piece of land lying opposite to the said Glass Works and called Williamson's Brick-bank . . . and also the Freehold land, Crate shops, Saggar Houses, Messuages, Dwelling houses or Tenements hereditaments and appurtenances known by the name of Middleport and extending from the Trent and Mersey Canal to the lane leading to Newport house . . . and also that slip of land near thereto and adjoining the said Canal with the Flint Ark and other buildings standing thereon . . . And being all the real property I am possessed of in the parish of Burslem aforesaid except my Newport House, Works and land purchased by me from Walter Daniel and a piece of land near thereto and adjoining to the lane leading to Newport House aforesaid purchased by me from Hugh Henshall Williamson and others—To such person and persons for such estates and in such manner as my son William Davenport shall by any deed or writing not Testamentary appoint and in default of appointment to him and his assigns for his life . . .

Because of the complications and alterations, affidavits had to be sworn by the witnesses concerning certain corrections, and the Will was endorsed on 12 May 1849; 'the Goods, Chattels and credits of the deceased within the province of Canterbury do not amount in value to One Hundred and twenty thousand Pounds, and that the Testator died on the twelfth day of December 1848.' He was buried at Leek Parish church.

The founder of the firm was dead. He had begun independent business during the lifetime of Josiah Wedgwood, he had seen his own concern outstrip that of his more-famous predecessor. He had been an active potter for over fifty years and one of his town's first Members of Parliament. He owned a country house and extensive amounts of land, he was undoubtedly a successful business-man. Moreover, in contrast to his son William, he knew the practical aspects of his business. He made some very fine pots. On occasions he evinced warmth towards his family, as on the eve of his sixty-seventh birthday when he sent Henry a present of oysters to celebrate and added, 'I hope they meet with a good tap of double XX to wash them down.' But such flashes of genuine humour are rare. We are entertained by the power of his invective, by his audacity and 'old-fashioned ways'. His portrait, reproduced on p 71, depicts a man of refined features, though the eyes are cold and the mouth firmly set. Simeon Shaw spoke of him as 'one of the most enterprizing and successful Manufacturers. Of his worth as a private person, the numerous instances of his benevolence are the best testimonials.' Unfortunately, few records of his benevolence survive. In a word, John Davenport did not radiate warmth. He was a hard, gritty capitalist; an 'old curmudgeon' certainly. Perhaps Miller's delicately phrased words will serve as fitting encomium: 'Of John Davenport it may be said that he was a man made for the circumstances and times in which he lived, and he was a man who made circumstances bend to his progress in life.'

During the 1840s and 1850s whilst the more unfortunate consequences of the Industrial Revolution were manifest at the Davenport factory, the day-to-day management seems to have devolved more and more upon managers and what C. Shaw called 'Bailees'. William Davenport increasingly lived the life of a country gentleman. He had succeeded his brother as MFH at Baddeley Edge, and was responsible in the 1840s for the revival of the North Staffs Hunt of which he was to be MFH for twenty-seven seasons (see C. J. Blagg, *A History of the North Staffordshire Hounds and Country 1825-1902* for details). At this period William was living at Longport Hall, a substantial early nineteenth century building just south of Trubshaw Cross in Longport. A print of the house as it looked in 1843 is reproduced in E. J. D. Warrilow, *A Sociological History of the City of Stoke-on-Trent*, p 295 (ii). The house was demolished in the 1880s. Later William moved to Maer.

John Davenport II lived at Westwood which,

in 1851, was extensively rebuilt. It is not known at what date John went to live permanently at Foxley, Herefordshire, though as he was High Sheriff of Staffordshire in 1854 it was almost certainly after this date. Six years after John's death in 1862 his sons, Rev G. H. Davenport and Harry Tichborne Davenport sold the Westwood estate to Mr John Robinson for about £50,000.

William Davenport, too, became High Sheriff of the county in 1859. Pre-occupation with country life does not appear, *initially*, to have hampered the progress of the firm. A remarkable document found recently and preserved at Hanley Museum gives us a fascinating glimpse of Davenport's foreign trade in the 1840s. As is clear from the text John Lockett of King St Longton was engaged in industrial espionage with the help of John Wardle and Davenport's bookkeeper at Liverpool:

Liverpool 17 Nov 1846.

John Lockett, Esq.

Dear Sir,

I enclose you a list of prices copied by Davenport bookkeeper from the last assortment they sent out to Ceylon, I find they have not sent any rice dishes very recently but the sizes in the list with prices are what have generally been sent out. You will perceive they invoice everything from the House at L'pool at 12 to the doz. and the same rule is adopted to all their houses of consignment. You will no doubt find the prices are such that will pay well. I know its unnecessary to request you will not say anything to Mr Fynn [Fynney] respecting the prices from Davenports.

I remain, Respectfully yours

John Wardle.

This particular list is not very informative, the wares being sent are Grecian bowls, muffins (small-sized plates), black-glazed oval teapots, butter tubs, sugars, creams, 'cow-shaped mugs' and 'bowls size 24 dipped, 1/9 for 12', etc. A further letter dated 25 April 1848 is much more interesting. Details of the services and pieces are quoted on p 66. The letter is worthy of reproduction in full:

Dear Sir,

The reason I have not answered your esteemed favour of 19th inst. sooner is I have been waiting opportunity to have access to Davenport's Sales Books and I now subjoin a copy of some adventures of theirs to the markets of Bombay, Calcutta & Madras. I find they are very similar assortments sent to each of those markets.

In the middle of the lists one reads: 'the above is the entire assortment of their last recent shipment, they sent twenty hogsheads.' Wardle ends:

I find they do not send any Willow ware, Persian painted or Cream Color'd ware to any of those markets or Tappies, but I think Tappies or Rice Dishes light blue P'd would take there, I ascertained Davenport have not yet made any consignments to these markets but what they have sent has either been thro' a merchant here that wanted freight or thro' a captain that could be depended upon and accustomed to those markets, and they divide profits with Davenports but the prices given with the discounts given is how they are invoiced to them, I understand as soon as the vessel arrives out the goods are sent to the public sale rooms and if the assortments are made up suitable there is generally good sales for them, I would especially point out to your notice that they do not like any patterns with human figures, animals or landscape patterns, such patterns as plants, flowers, chintzs or anything of bold in stripes or plaids would find more ready sales. The last shipment but one Davenports made to Bombay they sent 2 Dinner sets quantity as given of E'ware best white glaze with 2 gold lines, also 2 Dinner sets E'ware filled in & 1 H'hd of Breakfast & Tea ware white & gold. I always noticed when I have been waiting on any Gent. from Bombay that has been making a selection of goods for his own use or for his private speculations they mostly prefer'd the plain white & gold ware, some plain blue chintz patt'ns saying that those patt'ns looked cool for a warm climate.

If there is any information I have omitted if you will have the goodness to point it out, I will endeavour to get it for you, indeed I trust you will not hesitate to make use of me in any way I can be of service to you & as to your kind allusion to reciprocate I need not tell you that you have done so already on many occasions already, with much respect I remain

Dear sir

Very truly yours

John Wardle.

Trade with Canada and the United States continued and expanded in the forties and fifties. Mrs Collard has noted: 'In Montreal big sales of Davenport wares used to take place on the wharf by the ship's side.' Two such sales are mentioned. On 14 June 1851 the *Montreal Gazette* advertised a sale to take place 'alongside the brig BRITONS PRIDE of 50 crates assorted earthenware from the well-known house of William Davenport & Co of Liverpool.' Later in the same year the CITY OF MANCHESTER put in at Montreal and a sale was held of 64 crates and H'hds assorted earthenware all from the well-known firm of WILLIAM DAVENPORT & CO (Elizabeth Collard, pp 243-4).

Trade must have expanded on the Continent too, for, though there is no mention of it in the *Foxley* papers, a warehouse was in existence in Lübeck in 1840. A billhead illustrated in Godden's *Encyclopaedia*, p 116, dated 14 January 1840, has as one of the firm's addresses, 221 Schüsselbuden, Lübeck.

It is regrettable that, as yet, no trading figures or factory ledgers have come to light for this period of the firm's history. Thus we are left to speculate that after high success in the forties and early fifties, there was a decline in the fortunes of the firm. There is at present no proof of this. Straws in the wind maybe, such as the statement by Jewitt that manufacture at the Newport pottery 'was carried on by Messrs Cork & Edge'. Geoffrey Godden gives the date 1846 for the start of this enterprise (Godden, *Marks*, p 174). This may account for the exception made by John Davenport of this property in his will. At all events the Newport Works seems to have been given up as a Davenport manufactory. But until further research reveals the true state of affairs one can only say that to all outward appearances William Davenport was a most successful and affluent manufacturer. He had a high position in local society. In May 1854 he laid the foundation stone of the new—and third—Burslem Town Hall. This remarkable edifice still stands, and is still surmounted by the gilded angel (supporting a bird's nest) which so fascinated Arnold Bennett. William Davenport also gave a new organ to the Town Hall in 1864 (*VCH*, Vol VIII, p 112, footnote 75).

Yet all could not have been well. His estates, the Hunt—all were extremely expensive, and though he continued to purchase land and shares (for example, in 1857, he purchased Lees Farm for £14,600) his affairs were complicated. Much of his property including Lees Farm was later mortgaged. Details of these transactions are not known and can only be gleaned retrospectively from the *Wood* papers. What they make clear is that William Davenport's son Henry inherited very considerable financial difficulties.

It is to be hoped that this gap in the factory's history can be filled, until such a time, it may simply be recorded that William Davenport died in 1869. All the commentators agree that he had lost touch with the management of the firm, and that his pre-occupation with other matters had damaged the concern. Even if we do not accept all C. Shaw's emotional judgments about the man who drove his father to the workhouse and about 'how Nemesis has worked since', it would be hard to defend William Davenport in human terms. He is not a sympathetic figure.

The Problems of Affluence (1869-1887) Henry Davenport and Davenports Limited

The *Wood* papers which provide the documentary evidence for the last years of the life of the Davenport Pottery, are basically a collection of letters addressed to Edmund T. Wedgwood Wood, brother of Mrs William Davenport, by the Newcastle solicitor S. Herbert Cooper. Additionally Wood retained a few letters from other members of the family and certain more formal documents which will be referred to later. The letters cover the years 1877-86 and take us into the world of the Victorian middle class, a world of Consols, stock, entails and trustees, marriage settlements and liabilities—Forsyte territory. Much of this voluminous and fascinating correspondence is irrelevant to the main thread of the history of the potting concern and is thus omitted.

It is manifest from the first that William Davenport's legacy to his only son Henry had been a burden of Trusts, Mortgages and debts. A document of 23 April 1878 drawn up by Cooper (one of the Trustees) details the mortgage situation. The property which made up the 1869 'Longport' mortgage as it was called, was valued at £83,840 10s, of which £45,620 was the amount originally secured by the mortgage. The statement shows that since 1869 two major auction sales of property (in 1874 and 1876) had been held, as well as incidental small plots of land. The most important item was the sale of the Lower Bridge Pottery and 13,149 square yards of land, sold to Edward Clarke & Co in 1876 for £7,500. Other items included the Duke of Bridgewater Inn (£1,975), the Greyhound Inn (£1,100) and land and property at Wolstanton, Longport, Newport and in Burslem itself. The totals of all these sales came to £42,767 11s 7d, but further mortgage repayments and payments to the Trustees of two of William Davenport's married daughters of their inheritance, meant that in 1878 the 'Longport' mortgage debt was still £29,691 1s 5d.

Towards the end of 1877 and early in 1878, Henry Davenport was trying to dispose of the remainder of the Longport concern. A valuation was made on 6 December 1877. The major items were:

Longport Stock	
Earthenware & China	10,771. 0.10
Stock at Bridge Works	3,845.15. 9
Glass Works—Glass	1,838. 6. 6
	16,455.13. 1.
Utensils, materials etc at Longport, Bridge and Glass Works	18,144.16. 1
Freehold Longport Works, Glass Works Water supply and Shord tip Newport	28,085. 7. 0
The total with other sundry items	75,426. 9. 8
In addition:	
London Stock	20,294. 4. 3.
Fixtures	1,201.16. 6
Lease	3,245. 0. 0
	24,741. 0. 0
Liverpool Stock	15,244.16. 8
Fixtures and lease	15,000. 0. 0
	30,244.16. 8

The final total with other sundries £131,312. 7. 1.

As we shall see subsequently this was a considerable over-valuation in certain respects. But Henry Davenport writing from Newport to his uncle—E. T. W. Wood—optimistically enquired whether he should ask £150,000 for the entire concern, or 'whether you think I am *not* sacrificing too much by putting it at £131,312 7s 1d and deduct £5,000' (for shares which he would take himself) (*Wood* papers, 6 Dec 1877).

The prospective purchaser of the concern was David Chadwick, MP. But nothing came of this negotiation and Henry Davenport sank deeper into debt during 1878-9.

Meanwhile, the Pottery continued manufacture and wares were sent to London and Liverpool and thence exported, though as there is no mention anywhere in the *Wood* papers of a Hamburg house, this must have been given up some years previously. Whether the workers knew of their employer's situation cannot be determined, but they must have been aware that parts of the property were on offer and realised that there were financial difficulties. By the summer of 1879, it must have been common knowledge that all was not well. On 18 June at Burslem, Longport Hall, for many years the occasional residence of John and William Davenport, was sold. The Hall and a piece of land realised £4,700. They were bought by a Mr Hook whose intention seems to have been 'to re-sell to the town of Burslem for the purpose of a Cottage Hospital'. Longport *House* was not sold, and as Cooper reported to Wood on 19 June 1879:

> This state of things will disappoint & I believe annoy the Bank, who have been led (not by me) to expect a considerable reduction in their overdraft & thus a conflict may arise between them & the Trustees of Mr Davenport's will as to the destination of the purchase money for the Hall, which is to be paid at Michaelmas next—
>
> The Trustees will be anxious to meet Mr Henry's wishes as far as possible, but their first duty is to the Ladies, & before allowing any

part of the purchase money to go in relief of the Bank overdraft, they should be satisfied of their own position & of the ample sufficiency of the security they still retain . . .

'The Ladies' in question were the three younger, spinster daughters of William Davenport who had not received their 'fortunes' under his Will of ten years earlier. Less than a week later Cooper had to report: 'Mr Hook's cheque with which he paid the deposit on the purchase of Longport Hall has been dishonoured' (*Wood*, 24 June 1879). This was a blow and it was agreed that not much more could be done until trade revived.

By December, Cooper was urging action 'in order to meet the pressing requirements of the Bank' (*Wood*, 8 Dec 1879). However, assistance appeared to be on hand as Mr Chadwick had renewed his interest in the concern and 'is prepared to form the Longport Works into a Limited Liability Co' (*Wood*, 3 Jan 1880). Henry Davenport's relief is obvious when he writes to Wood on 5 January: 'I am quite relieved to get out. It will be much better for me to do so & pay off as many of my liabilities as I can.' But he evinced no sense of urgency about meeting Chadwick, and Cooper writing in his own hand a letter marked *Private* reported on 28 January:

> I have said to him—'I cannot exaggerate the critical nature of your position, altho' I fear you will not believe me, & I am satisfied that nothing but the most prompt & businesslike action on your part can arrest a Catastrophy.'

Rather ominously he adds:

> I am sorry to say however that both at Longport, London and Liverpool there seems to be a general desire to postpone the Auditor's visit.

He continues that some preliminary figures will have to be supplied:

> . . . Otherwise while the auditors are struggling [against much opposition] to complete a Balance Sheet, Mr Henry will find himself ruined.
>
> The Bank is most pressing and hostile in its tone . . . I am too aware of . . . urgent demands, while I cannot but feel that one single writ, issued by any one & for even a comparatively small amount, might involve a petition in Bankruptcy.
>
> Mr Henry does not appear to appreciate his position; strongly as I have spoken & written to him on the subject, & now I feel that two courses only are open to me—one is to carry out, under your advice, the sale that has been agreed to & the other is to ask Mr Henry to seek professional advice elsewhere.

The negotiations dragged on. Chadwick asked for satisfaction on six specific points. The documents went to and fro, Chadwick noted to Cooper that 'the working of the entire business for the last eighteen months appears to have resulted in a loss of £3,173.' He also strongly recommended the separation of the Longport and Liverpool businesses (*Wood*, 26 April 1880).

Chadwick's lukewarm attitude is reflected in Cooper's letter of 29 April 1880, again in his own hand and marked *Private:*

> I wrote you hurriedly yesterday to relieve your anxiety as to the wages for Saturday next . . .
>
> You will see how severe the tention (*sic*) is at Longport & I cannot feel any great confidence in the result of Mr Chadwick's mission—indeed he does not appear to be very sanguine himself, as the enclosed copy letter will show you.
>
> I am therefore taking upon myself to make some private enquiries for a purchaser, for the result will be fatal if we come to the end of the three months loan given by the bank & they find that nothing has been done.
>
> In the meantime I am urging Mr Henry to dispose of Liverpool & let Maer without delay & I trust you will do & say all you can to second my advice if you approve, & if you do not tell me what other steps you recommend. . .

Chadwick's advice to separate Longport and Liverpool did not appeal to John Shirley and Mr Mawdesley the managers most closely concerned. 'They speak of Liverpool as Longport's best customer,' Cooper noted. Again on 4 May Cooper is pessimistic: 'I do not feel very sanguine as to Mr Chadwick's success, and my thoughts have been much occupied lately in devising an alternative scheme to which Mr Henry may turn' [and so save himself from the threatened proceedings by the Bank] 'if Mr Chadwick's prove abortive.'

The three months the Bank had given Chadwick to form a Company had nearly expired and a further extension was required during which

Wood was requested to pen a letter which might be shown to interested parties. It was stipulated that the following statement be included: 'That the terms of the proposed purchase are fair and reasonable and that the price to be paid for the stock will leave a sufficient and ample margin of profit over and above all expenses of sale or management' (*Wood*, 24 May 1880).

Mr Shirley the Longport manager provided a similar letter and agreed to put £5,000 in the new Company. A prospectus was prepared for Davenports Limited to purchase from the sole proprietor Mr Henry Davenport 'the entire business and connection of Messrs William Davenport & Co one of the oldest and most celebrated manufacturers of China, Earthenware and Glass'. The capital was to be £60,000 divided into 3,000 seven percent preference shares at £10 each, and 3,000 ordinary shares also at £10 each. Henry Davenport and his friends were to take up £15,000 of the shares, and a purchase price of £5,000 was fixed for a portion of the stock at Liverpool and £25,000 for the Longport Works. The lease of the latter would include:

> Landlord's fixtures of the estimated value of £9,587 a dwelling house and four cottages adjoining the manufactory—a Crate shop, Saggar house and pools [which supply the water required on the Works] adjacent thereto and a Schraff tip at Middleport which contains an available area of upwards of six acres. . .

The showrooms and agency at Ely Place, Holborn, London, were also included. (Obviously, at an unrecorded date the Fleet Street showrooms had been vacated.)

Wood in his letter of recommendation dated 28 May 1880 had stressed that the firm's goods 'are well-known in every foreign market', and he added an important personal note concerning Henry Davenport:

> I think you know the circumstances under which Mr Henry Davenport is parting with the business. His father who realised a large fortune by it never intended him to continue in it—he was not brought up to it—he neither understands or (*sic*) cares for it, and in my judgement he will do well to dispose of it even at the very low figure mentioned in the prospectus, for he has no children, and no near relative able to take the concern off his hands. (*Wood*, E. T. W. Wood to D. Chadwick, MP.)

All looked set fair for a sale, but on 1 June Cooper wrote to Wood in some agitation. It appears, not to mince words, that the books had been tampered with and a false prospectus presented:

> The following, which has just come to my knowledge, will confirm to your mind the suspicion with which we have always looked upon the valuation of Stock &c in the Longport Balance Sheet & appears to me to call for some adjustment of figures with Mr Chadwick . . . When the long resisted audit by Deloitte & Co became inevitable these items [value of engravings, moulds and utensils] were for the purpose of the Balance Sheet altered . . . Thus a loss of £8,553 was concealed . . . This announcement at the present juncture places us in an awkward position with Mr Chadwick & I strongly recommend Mr Henry to make some reduction in the £25,000 & so meet the difficulty at once . . .

The whole transaction was now in jeopardy. Especially as Cooper noted on 11 June that the National Provincial Bank was unhappy at the reduction in valuation of Longport and at the proposed purchase price; for, 'after paying all debts and other charges upon the business . . . there will only be about £8,000 to go to the Bank, and they object to the payment of other creditors in full while they receive a comparatively small part of their debt; for the overdraft at the present time is close upon £30,000.' The alternative which the Bank had made plain to Cooper was for them 'to pay the Ladies off, and having thus taken everything into their own hands, to break Mr Henry up and know the worst of their position'.

Unfortunately, there seems to be a gap in the correspondence at this point and the outcome is not precisely documented. What can be positively stated is that Chadwick did not purchase the business, and Mr Henry was not 'broken up'.

In September he must have obtained some relief for he sold his 'reversionary share in the residual personal estate of the late Mr John Wood now represented by the sum of £66,591 4s 10d Consols, to Mr Mountford Wood' (*Wood*, 13 September 1880). Further good news was forthcoming on 3 January 1881 when Cooper was happy to announce that 'I have sold the Top Bridge

Works to Mr T. Hughes for £3,100, the purchase to be completed on 25 March next.' The purchase price was to be taken by the Trustees for the Ladies in part discharge of their mortgage. (All the daughters of William Davenport had been left £5,374 5s 8d. The married daughters had in due course received their 'fortunes', but the four unmarried ones had not and Miss Jessie's marriage to Col Buller was being held up until payment was made. In May 1881, Cooper suggested payment in cash 'to stop enquiry into Mr Henry's affairs on the part of Col Buller's Solicitor—it would look better.' The money would be given to her Trustees by her late father's Trustees.)

Later in the same month a sale of 'the first portion of the very valuable stock of China, cut glass services and Beautiful Ornaments' took place over five days at Canning Place, Liverpool. The auctioneers compiled a catalogue of some 1,200 lots, a copy of which is in the *Wood* papers. No prices are recorded, and many of the wares sold were not of Davenport manufacture. Thus the value of the catalogue as a source of information on the types of ware being produced in these later years is very limited.

Though he was not out of trouble yet, Mr Henry received this tribute on 17 May 1881 from Cooper: 'I cannot say too strongly how satisfied I have felt at the care and consideration Mr Henry has shown since July last, and at the loyal manner in which he has adhered to the task he then set himself . . .'

Further relief was at hand, for the ever-diligent Cooper had prepared a scheme for the formation of 'a private company for taking over the Works'. By 21 July 1881, Cooper had prepared an agreement for the sale of the Works to the proposed company, had drawn up a Memorandum & Articles of Association, and secured promises to take shares from friends and relatives with the exception of a mere £1,000 worth of shares. The whole transaction had been accomplished much more smoothly than any of the previous rather fraught negotiations.

All the anxieties and worries were now to be put aside. The formal conclusion of the business was to be conducted in a manner befitting Victorian gentlemen of property:

> . . . There is to be a Family gathering at Queen Anne's Mansions on Wednesday next from 4 to 7 at which I have no doubt you will be present. Mr H. T. Davenport has suggested that the members of the family interested in the Company might arrange to adjourn from the meeting either to the House of Commons, or some convenient place in the neighbourhood, where the Memorandum and Articles of Association may be signed by the requisite number [7] (*Wood*, Cooper to Wood, 21 July 1881).

Further delays and doubts as to whether £10,000 additional capital was sufficient to carry on the Works protracted matters until eventually on 9 August 1881 the new Company of Davenports Limited was formed. The capital of the company was £40,000 and the members of the family who signed the Memorandum of Association were:

DIANA ELIZABETH DAVENPORT, Camp Hill Newcastle-under-Lyne, Staffre, *Spinster*.

SARAH E. DAVENPORT, Camp Hill Newcastle-under-Lyne, Staffre, *Spinster*.

MARIANNE H. DAVENPORT, Camp Hill, Newcastle-under-Lyne, Staffre, *Spinster*.

HARRY T. DAVENPORT, MP, Hem Heath, Trentham, Staffre.

R. MOUNTFORD WOOD, Albury Rectory, Tring, *Clerk in Holy Orders*.

GEORGE W. WOOD *Major*, Warley, Brentwood, Essex.

GEORGE H. DAVENPORT, Foxley, Hereford, *Clerk in Holy Orders*.

There were to be five Directors, the first to be E. T. W. Wood of Henley Hall, Salop, H. T. Davenport, MP, Major G. W. Wood, 'Mr Alfred Henry Dashwood, formerly of Stamford Hall, Leicester now of Longport, Gentleman' and one other to be nominated by the named four.

The declared objects of the company, nine in all, are too lengthy to be quoted here, but the company was to act as both Manufacturer and Dealer in a whole list of ceramic wares, and was to acquire all Henry Davenport's Longport concerns still used by the Pottery.

Understandably, the Cooper-Wood correspondence diminishes in volume after the hectic activity prior to the formation of what was clearly a much smaller enterprise than it had been in the heyday of William Davenport. In fact, with the Newport pottery sold or leased, and with the Top Bridge and Bottom Bridge potteries gone, the concern had returned to the size of eighty years previously. Davenports Limited was confined to

John Davenport's original Unicorn Bank Longport and the Glass works.

Initially, all went well. The first annual balance sheet which ran from 1 July 1881 to 5 August 1882 showed a gross profit of £6,997 12s 2½d. After payment of a dividend and other adjustments, a balance of £4,649 18s 4½d was carried forward to the following year. This first balance sheet—preserved at Hanley with the *Wood* papers—is interesting as an indication of the scale of operation of the firm. The value of ware manufactured was £54,859 15s 4d; the stock of china, earthenware and glass held at Longport was valued at £8,814 2s 1d; the materials at £5,537 17s 7d; the engravings at £1,890 19s 7d; the blocks, cases and moulds at £1,811 15s 0d; utensils at £5,151 11s 3d; machinery, presses, pumps, furnace, boats, etc at £6,267 and fixtures at the London agency at £300. In addition there were stocks of china, earthenware and glass at Liverpool of £8,828 and fittings in the Lord Street shop of £462 2s 2d. Altogether the company, though reduced in size, was still by any standards in the potting industry, a large undertaking. Unfortunately, we have no record of the number of people employed at this date.

There seems to have been no real relief financially for Henry Davenport, for we read in the correspondence that Mr J. B. Wood was holding Plate as a security for a loan (*Wood*, 16 Dec 1882).

The 1883 balance sheet contains an ominous sentence about 'the late depression of trade'. Although there was a working profit of £1,742, a loss of £541 was reported on the New York agency and after a dividend payment of £1,400 a much reduced balance of £2,474 19s 8d was carried forward. The significant figures are the increased value of stocks at both Longport and Liverpool (over £10,000 worth in total at each place) and the decrease to £46,573 16s 0d in the value of the ware manufactured. To add to the difficulties, there had been a fire on the premises (*Wood*, 12 July 1883). Fortunately, insurance of £816 10s was recovered.

The General Manager, John Shirley seems to have been a sanguine character. Throughout the *Wood* papers, his reports are always optimistic and in November 1883 he informed clients from the London showroom address of 32 Ely Place EC that a Mr John Morgan had been engaged as an additional representative with 'a view to increasing . . . our Home Trade'.

In retrospect we can see that these are desperate measures. Most of the Directors had no real interest, other than financial, in the concern. If it lost money they would leave. The former owner, Henry Davenport still owed his father's Trustees over £14,000 in 1884, and the security for this was mortgaged property in which he had no particular interest. He still owed his bankers £10,000 and though it was reported that 'Henry himself has certainly tried to live on a small income', his father's legacy and his own early imprudence were insuperable obstacles to solvency.

The concern, too, was in difficulties, the 1884 balance sheet revealed a working loss of £4,388 11s 4d, a loss on consignments to New York and Pernambuco of £284, and a total loss of £6,338 2s 2d. Henry Davenport could expect no relief from that quarter! Stocks at Longport were now nearly £12,000, whilst the value of ware manufactured was further reduced to £34,081 9s. 8d. The loss according to the Directors 'is easily accounted for by the extra-ordinary depression in the Pottery Industry since May 1883'.

By the end of the year 1884, the selling of Maer had been seriously suggested. H. T. Davenport (John Davenport II's son) wrote to Wood on 15 December 1884: 'It is very sad to remember the good times we have had there, and the end of it all—luckily the present generation is the only one to suffer.' Cooper, who had been financing Henry Davenport for some time clearly felt he had done enough. On 17 December he informed Wood that 'The Bank is annoyed . . . and insist upon charging 3 percent on the overdraft for the current year.' He retains sufficient loyalty to urge: 'I need not tell you what must be the inevitable result of borrowing from the Jews—I am sorry . . . that Mr Henry has suggested such a step.' Thus the pottery and its former owner staggered from crisis to crisis.

The 1885 balance sheet brought no joy to either. 'The great depression in the Potting Trade has continued throughout the past year,' the Directors reported. The loss at Longport was £4,434 8s 6d; on the New York agency £751 19s 3d; only Liverpool made a slight profit. The overall loss was £6,262 14s 1d; stocks at Longport were higher than ever at £13,359 12s 7d, and the value of ware made had risen to £39,229 3s 11d. Despite these depressing statistics the Directors felt that 'another attempt should be made to keep the company on foot'. Cooper reported to Wood the results of conversations with H. T. Davenport and Dashwood on 3 October 1885:

> . . . It was thought that the present is not the time to wind up the Company, and that even if a sale of the business be decided upon, it should first be put in order for sale, so as to make the best of it in the interests of all concerned. A return of trade in the District might enable the Directors to dispose of the business as a going concern, which certainly could not be done now. It was thought that Spring is the time to sell, and in any case the Works should be carried on till then, and that this might at all events be done without a loss.

H. T. Davenport had agreed to raise a further £2,000 on a Debenture to keep the Company going, but there were technical difficulties in this, for were the money paid unconditionally into the Bank, it would simply be annexed to pay off—in part—the company's overdraft. These difficulties were overcome and potting continued, though only with the object of waiting for a more opportune time to sell the firm as a going concern.

Meanwhile, Henry Davenport and his sisters had at last resolved to sell the Maer estate, though Camp Hill the residence of the Ladies was to be excluded. Maer was to be offered for sale at Auction in the summer of 1886. An estimate of its potential worth is contained in some jotted notes on the back of a letter dated 15 July 1886:

> Timber £15,000, Fixtures including organ £11,000, 1st Sept 3,042 acres. House £30,000, Woodland £10 per acre.

The sale of Maer represented the end of an era for the Davenports. Already remote from the potbank upon which their family fortunes were founded, the sale of this their largest estate—symbolically purchased from the Wedgwoods at the apex of their success—was a token of their defeat.

Work continued at the factory during the period of H. T. Davenport's further investment. Unfortunately, there is no 1886 balance sheet in the *Wood* papers, but it is clear that further property sales took place in July 1886. The last letter noted in the series records the sale of ten plots of building land, but no sale for Longport House. The aggregate purchase money of land 'recently sold, including Pickford's Wharf amounts to £3,230 7s 10d'. More land was sold subsequently, and though the exact date at which manufacture ceased has not been established, an advertisement in the *Pottery Gazette* dated 1 December 1887 (p 1,185) gives a good approximation:

> There is to be an extensive sale of potters' utensils and materials etc. on the estate of Davenports Ltd which is now come to a full stoppage. There is a very valuable collection of copper-plate engravings, which I have no doubt will be eagerly sought for, as no doubt a key to further orders from some of Davenports Ltd former clients. There is at present no possibility of an ultimate recommencement of the works.

A supplement to the same journal dated 1 Feb 1888 notes that 'Mr A. Wenger, Helvetia Works, Hanley had purchased a large number of the copper plates'. Later in the same issue (*Pottery Gazette*, p 162) it is reported that 'the whole of the works have been purchased by Thomas Hughes of the Top Bridge Pottery, Longport . . . he has advertised the glass works to let.' In October, John Hughes of Cobridge called attention to his purchase of 'the whole of the valuable pattern books belonging to the late firm of Davenports Ltd' (*Pottery Gazette*, 1 Oct 1888). The same journal reported on 1 November 1889 that 'Mr Thomas Hughes has moved to the very extensive factory, lately occupied by Davenports Ltd.' Finally Geoffrey Godden records the Unicorn Pottery Longport remaining in the occupation of Thomas Hughes & Son (Ltd) until 1957, it was then taken over by Arthur Wood & Sons, but for a short time only. The buildings were demolished in 1961, though a few forlorn remnants lingered a little longer.

And so in 1887 the name of Davenport passed from the pottery world in which it had been so prominent for almost a century. That *Davenport* is worthy of study nearly a further century later is a tribute to the quality of the pots produced. The best of these—marked with the name of that remarkable family—were as good in quality in the last days as they had been in the beginning.

PART TWO: THE WARES

Cream-Coloured Earthenware

When John Davenport purchased the Unicorn Bank in 1794, the staple product of the Staffordshire potters was cream-coloured earthenware. The evolution and adaptation of this body and its perfection by Josiah Wedgwood in the early 1760s need not detain us (see D. Towner, pp 1-9, 33-4). The exploitation of this fine, light, durable and cheap product by John Baddeley, John Turner, the Leeds Pottery and a host of other potters was already by 1794 an almost-completed chapter in the history of English ceramics. In a word, by 1794, creamware was becoming old-fashioned. This point is worth stressing for Davenport's creamware is not particularly distinguished. We look in vain for the wonderful tea and coffee pots of Wedgwood and his Staffordshire rivals. The elaborately pierced chestnut baskets of the Leeds potters find no place in the repertoire of Davenport. His ware is simple, stylish in an unobtrusive way, and saleable.

The body of creamware had stabilised throughout the late eighteenth century and consisted of china clay, china stone, flint and ball clay. The proportions varied from potter to potter, as did the elements which composed the glaze which gave the ware its colour. There is no record of the various recipes used by John Davenport, but the product is much like that of his fellow-potters. Light in weight, pale cream in colour, the ware is pleasant to handle and use. Glaze colour varies somewhat, but where it lies thickly—as it does under the base of the comport (5)—it may show a greenish hue.

Davenport creamware is not particularly plentiful. Pieces such as the dishes decorated by William Absolon (1) are met with very rarely indeed. Absolon set up a decorating establishment in Yarmouth in about 1790, and here he painted wares bought 'in the white' from Staffordshire and Yorkshire potteries (Mankowitz and Haggar, pp 1-2). A marked plate painted by Absolon with a 'Round Leaf'd Rest Harrow' copied from Curtis's *Botanical Magazine* is in the Harris Museum collection, Preston. Absolon had no direct connec-

1a and b *(above) Creamware side dishes.*
Left: Lobed oval dish painted in sepia touched with green. The border lines in green. The flowers are named on the back 'Pasque Flower'.
Length 10½in. Mark: No 2 and painted in sepia 'Absolon Yarm[th] *No 25'.*
Right: Rectangular-shaped dish painted in sepia with a flower spray named on the back 'Arbae a Fratex'.
The border lines in green.
Length 8in. Mark: No 2 and painted in sepia 'Absolon Yarm[th]*'. Both date from c 1800-10.*
Victoria and Albert Museum

2 *(below) Creamware plates with simple border patterns.*
Left to right: (i) Plate with border enamelled in a complex geometric pattern in brown, yellow, red and blue.
Diam 8¼in. No mark (see p 34). Pattern number 138. Date: c 1795-1805.
(ii) Plate with border pattern of a repeated yellow leaf and three-fruit motif enamelled on a grey-green ground within a brown border.
Diam 7¾in. Mark: No 1. No pattern number. Date: c 1800-10.
(iii) Plate with pierced rim which is decorated with a border pattern of trailing leaves in red, set between two brown lines.
Diam 7½in. Mark: No 2. No pattern number. Date: c 1800-10.
(iv) Plate with enamelled border decoration of black lines and dots enclosing a yellow band painted with a black leaf motif.
Diam 8¼in. No mark (see p 34). Pattern number 177. Date: c 1805.

tion with the factory as far as is known. He purchased Davenport wares—and those of other factories—to paint upon.

The normal factory decoration consisted of a simple border pattern in the Wedgwood style. The four plates (2) show a range of such patterns, and amongst them are two of only three pieces illustrated in this book which are unmarked. The authentication of (2 iv), pattern 177, is provided by a most interesting pair of creamware pattern plates depicted in G. A. Godden's *Encyclopaedia*, plate 192. Each plate is painted with six different and numbered border patterns, amongst which pattern 177 is clearly identical with that shown in (2). The pattern range shown on the plates is not consecutive. One has patterns in the 59-67 range, the other 169-184. Pattern 177 is of particular interest as it is almost identical with a Wedgwood pattern. The other attributed plate is (2 i), pattern 138. It has an identical profile to that of pattern 177 and matches it in body weight, general colour and glaze. The pierced plate (2 iii) is marked but has no pattern number, but a similar piece with a floral border was of pattern 253. This latter is almost the highest creamware pattern noted. A large, marked soup tureen with the usual leaf-stye border pattern, modelled in a typical Wedgwood smooth oval shape had pattern number 275 painted upon it.

Unfortunately, many of the most attractive patterns seem not to have been given a number. The very pleasing pattern on the plate (2 ii), which also occurs on the tureen (3), the basket and stand (4) and the castor or draining ladle (5), is without a number. One can only assume—leaving aside negligence—that either the pattern was so well-known in the factory that it required no number to identify it, or that it was designed and in use for some time before any pattern book was put together. Incidentally, there is no trace of any of the Davenport pattern books.

We can conclude that a goodly number of the marked creamwares bore no pattern number for, additionally to the above, the comport and dish (5), the tureen (4) and the very attractive side-dish (8) also have none. Of the pattern numbers recorded, 275 is highest; lowest is 59 which appears on the pattern plate illustrated by Godden.

It must be emphasised that the pattern number refers to the decoration, usually a border pattern

3 *(above) Two creamware sauce tureens.*
Left: Tureen and cover with 'twisted rope' handles and a curled knop. Painted with a conventional border pattern in shades of green. The tureen and stand are joined as one piece and the underside of the base is hollow up to the point where it meets the tureen.
Total height $6\frac{1}{2}$*in. Overall length 7in. Mark: No 2. No pattern number. Date: c 1795-1805.*
Right: Tureen and cover (stand attached as above) painted with a border pattern of a repeated yellow leaf and three-fruit motif on a grey-green ground within a border of brown lines.
Dimensions as above. Mark: No 1. No pattern number. Date: c 1800-10.

4 *(below) Creamware pierced dessert basket and stand.*
Basket pierced to within $1\frac{1}{8}$*in of the rim which is decorated inside with a border pattern as on plate 2 (ii). Shaped loop handle with one spur on the outside and one inside.*
Overall length $10\frac{3}{8}$*in. Width 7in. Height 3in. Mark: No 1. No pattern number. Date: c 1800-10. This piece bears a printed label with the words, 'Leeds Exhibition 1875. Property of Mr Roberts. No 11'.*
Stand for the above, with pierced rim, similarly decorated.
Length $10\frac{1}{4}$*in. Width* $7\frac{3}{4}$*in. Mark, pattern and date as on the basket.*

on the creamwares, and has no relationship to the shape of the object. It is purely the concern of the decorator and facilitates both the ordering and production of the wares.

The Davenports were always a 'commercial' factory, and it is unlikely that they ever strayed into the field of creamware figures. Indeed, even teawares have not been noted in pure creamware (see pp 44-5). Dessert wares predominate and representative shapes are depicted in the illustrations for the guidance of collectors. The shapes are generally simple and elegant in keeping with the restraints imposed by the neo-classical style which still affected the artistic climate of the period. The more elaborate, moulded wares such as the tureen (7) are later and seem to date from the end of the true creamware period. The piece illustrated is noticeably whiter in finish. It too has no pattern number, though a similarly moulded and decorated service bore the number 135, which may serve as a reminder that a comparatively low pattern number does not always indicate an early date. Some patterns such as these botanical paintings remained popular for many years. The dessert plate (6) also appears to be a slightly later piece. It bears no pattern number, but the attractive enamel painting is reminiscent of the chinoiserie on the early porcelain piece (63). Equally attractive was a part dessert service on display at the Hudson Historical Society Exhibition in 1969, of which the centrepiece bore a sepia-coloured painting of 'the East Front of Luxborough House in Essex, the seat of Sir Edward Hughes Bart'.

Other objects were fashioned in creamware such as bulb pots (8) of which a good example with dolphin-mask handles is in the Victoria & Albert Museum, and pot-pourri vases of which a magnificent example enamelled in sepia monochrome was illustrated in *The Connoisseur*, June 1967 p 116.

By 1810 or thereabouts most of the potteries were turning away from creamwares and producing pearl wares or plain white-body wares. All the evidence indicates that John Davenport did likewise. There is little true creamware that one could date to after 1815.

Finally, the marks. Not all creamware was marked by any means, though a good proportion appears to have been impressed with one or other of the marks shown on pp 110-1 as No 1 and No 2.

5 *(above) Creamware dessert comport, ladle and side dish.*
Left. Comport decorated with a broad border pattern of leaves alternately painted in red and green with brown outlines and border. Under the hollow foot a pool of greenish-coloured glaze has gathered.
Length 10½in. Width 7¾in. Height 4¾in. Mark: No 2. No pattern number. Date: c 1810-15.
Centre: Pierced draining ladle or sugar sifter. Decorated with brown enamel on handle and rims, and yellow leaf motif as (3 and 4).
Overall length 7½in. No mark. No pattern number. Date: c 1800-10.
Right: Side dish decorated as comport above.
Length 9½in. Max width 7in. Mark, pattern and date as above.

6 *(below left) Creamware plate.*
Plate decorated with coloured enamel painting of two seated Chinamen playing musical instruments. They are observed by two birds seated on branches which encircle the plate. The base is flat and the rim outward-curving.
Diam 7⅝in. Mark: No 2 and a star impressed. No pattern number. Date: c 1805-15.
Victoria and Albert Museum

7 *(below right) Creamware sauce tureen and stand.*
Tureen and cover elaborately moulded and shaped with a pattern of leaves. The rims are outlined in brown enamel and each side of the tureen and cover is painted with an English flower in full colour. The naturalistic knop is coloured green.
Overall length 7½in. Height (with lid) 6in.
The stand is separate and is enamelled with a blue convolvulus (morning glory). The moulded outline follows that of the tureen.
Length 9in. Width 6½in. Mark: No 2. No pattern number on either piece. Date: c 1805-15.
City of Liverpool Museum

White Stoneware

The jugs and mug (9) represent a typical sample of what must have been a large output of white stoneware vessels. These high-fired stonewares, usually decorated with a broad band of brown, or more occasionally bright blue, enamel colour on the rim and handle, enjoyed great popularity in the first two decades of the nineteenth century. They are transitional between the off-white or light cane-coloured stonewares of John Turner and the later stone china body. The white stoneware vessels were fully glazed within; outside they had a smear glaze or possibly only a thin coat of glaze which had 'flashed' from the glazed interior of the pots and saggars on to the outside of the wares during firing.

They are handsome, durable and slightly translucent, and of the three pieces depicted, the taller jug is the earliest and best modelled. The sprigged 'Huntsmen' scene is excellently done, and bears comparison with similar work by Spode, Adams, Enoch Wood and Wedgwood as well as many other potters who used the same design. The mug is rather later and comparatively weak in finish. The jug on the left is unusual in that it is coloured, and furthermore represents the less-common scene of 'The Stag Hunt'. The enamels are bright and lively, and although later than the taller jug, this piece is of greater rarity.

Mugs and jugs in the white stoneware continued to be made well into the 1820s and possibly later. As a general rule, the taller, more upright models are the earlier. Certain other articles, such as match pots (spill vases) were probably made in this body. Marks are impressed.

8 *(above) Creamware bulb pot and dessert side dish.*
Left: Bulb pot (pierced cover missing) with flat undecorated back and semi-circular front painted with large red dahlias and a mass of small red and green leaves. Crabstock handle painted in two shades of green.
Height 4½in. Width at top 5in. Front to back 4in. Mark: No 2. No pattern number. '19' impressed—probably a size number. Date: c 1810-20.
Right: Oval dessert dish with lobed and indented ends. The centre undecorated but stained through use. Border enamelled in pink, yellow and green with a trailing design of aquilegias framed by two black lines. Length 10½in. Width 7½in. Mark: No 2. No pattern number. Date: c 1795-1805.

9 *(below) White stoneware jugs and mug.*
Left: Stoneware jug, fully glazed within, slight glaze on the outside. The neck, base and top half of the handle enamelled in brown. On the body, applied relief decoration of scenes from 'The Stag Hunt'. A dismounted rider holding his horse raises his whip to hounds which are savaging the stag. Two other horsemen approach. The scene is flanked on either side by trees. The scene is enamelled in bright colours.
Height 6½in. Mark: No 3. Date: c 1810-20.
Centre: Stoneware mug, glazed within, smear glaze outside, decorated with a band of brown enamel on the rim and the top half of the handle. On the body, applied relief scenes of 'The Huntsmen'.
Height 3½in. Mark: No 3. Date: c 1820-30.
Right: Stoneware jug, fully glazed within, slight glaze on the outside. The neck and top half of the handle enamelled in brown. On the body, applied relief scenes of 'The Huntsmen'.
Height 7in. Mark: No 2. Date: c 1800-1810.

CANEWARE

Caneware, like the white stoneware, was a popular body in the early nineteenth century. Potters such as John Turner and Josiah Spode had produced this dry-body ware in considerable quantities and for a wide variety of useful and ornamental items. The Davenport canewares are amongst the most interesting of their early wares. They have a distinctive appeal not only to the eye but also to the touch.

Prominent are the decorative wine coolers. Certain recipes for the porous body are given by William Evans (pp 17-18). Evans also comments on their use: 'After being immersed in water till saturated, on any substance being placed therein, the cold caused by evaporation reduces the temperature of that substance to a most palatable state.'

The two coolers illustrated as (10) and (11 and 13) are of especial interest. The Hanley piece with its finely modelled portrait of Nelson and his naval trophies clearly dates from the first decade of the nineteenth century. The Liverpool example, one of a pair, with enamelled Egyptian motifs, is a reminder of the great interest aroused in Egyptian antiquities as a result of Napoleon's Egyptian campaign 1798-9. The 'Topers' cooler (12) may be somewhat later in date, it certainly has a more bucolic and English flavour.

All such wine coolers are exceedingly rare. Slightly more plentiful are jugs, finely finished with engine-turning and enamelled border patterns (17). Rather surprisingly, teawares were made in the caneware body. Recently, a set comprising a saucer, a cup of a beautifully rounded shape with simple loop handle and completely unglazed, a plate and a small coffee can glazed within, have come into the author's possession. Only the plate is marked, but the wares are *en suite*. A marked piece of caneware teaware with the name of the Irish china dealer DONOVAN (impressed) has also been reported.

The exigencies of the Napoleonic war forced up the price of wheat to extraordinary limits. The Staffordshire potters took to providing piecrust substitutes in caneware. Davenport not only produced the small individual pie dish shown in (15) but much larger covered dishes in the

10 *(above left) Dry body wine cooler.*
Light cane-coloured wine cooler, unglazed. Decorated in brown enamel with a 'Greek key' border pattern and a scene of Egyptian pictures and symbols. Handles in the form of open-mouthed dolphin masks. Height 9½in. Overall width 9½in. Mark: No 2 impressed twice. Date: c 1798-1808.
City of Liverpool Museum

11 *(above right) Dry body wine cooler.*
Cane-coloured wine cooler, unglazed. Moulded in high relief with oak leaves and acorns and a bust portrait of Admiral Lord Nelson. Handles in the form of Satyr's head.
Height 10in. Overall width 9¾in. Mark: No 2. Date: 1800-1810.
Hanley Museum, Stoke-on-Trent

12 *(below left) Dry body wine cooler.*
Dark cane-coloured body, unglazed. Moulded in relief with 'The Topers' who are seated at a table drinking and smoking. On the reverse, a similar scene with one of the figures slumped across the table. Trees and other foliage fill out the picture. Below, a broad band of engine-turned pattern. Handles in the form of open-mouthed dolphin masks.
Height 9in. Overall width 9in. Mark: No 2. Date: c 1800-15.
City of Liverpool Museum

13 *(below right) Dry body wine cooler.*
The reverse side of (11) above, moulded in high relief with naval trophies, an anchor, a ship, a sword, flags, etc.
Dimensions, mark and date as for (11).
Hanley Museum, Stoke-on-Trent

unglazed caneware were also made in the same form as the late piece (56). A slightly smaller example in Hanley Museum would appear to date from about 1805-10.

Lastly, the moulded basket (14) has the unusual feature of enamelled decoration which hardly seems in keeping with this fine-textured ware. Few pieces of the authentic unglazed caneware appear to have been made after 1820. Marks are impressed, normally in lower-case letters.

BLACK BASALT

More prolific in general than caneware is black basalt. This too is a form of high-fired, hard stoneware, stained throughout with manganese and iron, and brought to fine perfection by Josiah Wedgwood about 1766. It remained a popular body throughout the eighteenth century and during the first decades of the nineteenth. Indeed, it is still produced today. Davenport's basalt, however, is exceedingly rare, or rather marked pieces are. It is likely that their basalt was largely left unmarked. Marked basalt of any manufacture (other than Wedgwoods of a later date) is rare. For example, very few marked Spode basalt pieces are recorded.

Just three marked Davenport pieces are known to the author. A cream jug from Hanley Museum is illustrated (16), it would seem to date from c 1815-25. A bowl of about 6in diameter, decorated with moulded classical figures and engine-turning, has been noted. And recently, the author has acquired a small teapot, again with classical motifs and with a lid whose finial is in the well-known form of the seated and veiled female figure, sometimes referred to as 'the widow of Zarephath'. It is hoped to illustrate this piece and certain other unusual earthenware items in the *Transactions of the English Ceramic Circle* for 1973.

All the pieces bear the impressed mark No 3 (upper case letters) and do not seem to belong to the earliest years of the factory's production.

14 *(above left) Dry body circular basket.*
Small caneware basket and handle moulded with basket-weave. Glazed inside, decorated on the outside with a light wash of green enamel; base unglazed.
Diam (at top) $3\frac{1}{2}$in. Height (without handle) 2in. Total height $3\frac{3}{4}$in. Mark: No 2. Date: c 1800-10.
City of Liverpool Museum

15 *(above right) Dry body dish and cover.*
Small caneware circular dish and cover, crisply moulded to represent pastry. Glazed within, unglazed outside.
Diam of base $4\frac{1}{2}$in. Height $1\frac{1}{2}$in. Mark: No 2. Both lid and base have '17' impressed. The base alone has the word WARRENTED impressed. Date: c 1795-1810.
Hanley Museum, Stoke-on-Trent

16 *(below left) Black basalt cream jug.*
Basalt jug with a squat body decorated with an engine-turned design. The handle is square in profile, the lip full and wide.
Height $3\frac{1}{2}$in. Length (handle to spout) $4\frac{1}{2}$in. Mark: No 3. Date: 1815-25.
Hanley Museum, Stoke-on-Trent

17 *(below right) Dry body jug.*
Cane-coloured stoneware jug with engine-turned decoration at the base, a plain body and an enamelled border of harebells in blue and green leaves. Blue enamel lines decorate the rims and handle. Glazed inside only.
Height $5\frac{3}{4}$in. Mark: No 2. Date: c 1800-10.

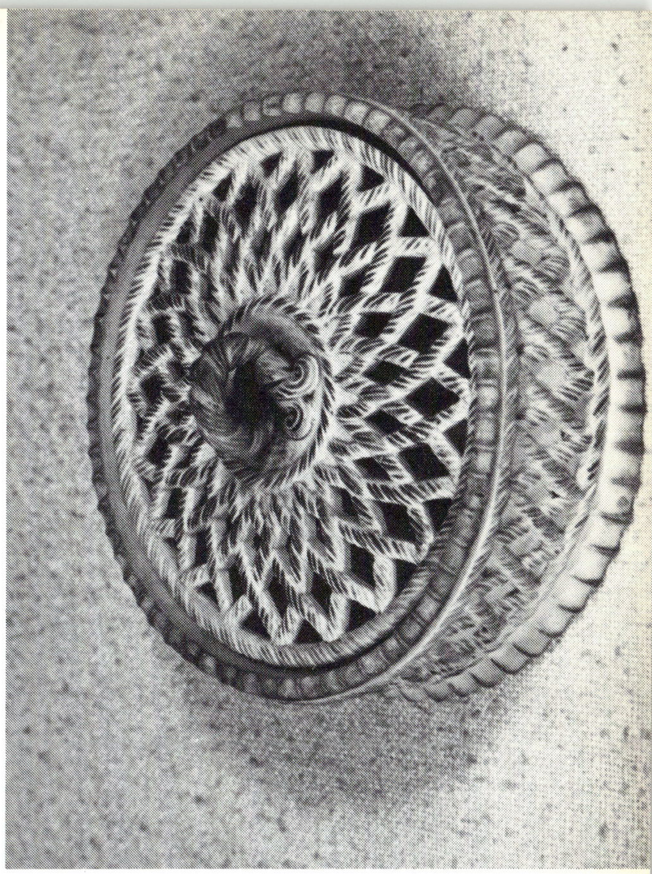

Coloured-Body Earthenwares

A very distinctive class of wares was produced at Davenports during some period of the first twenty-five years of the factory's existence. This is a coloured-body earthenware, not in the usual drab or grey shades, but in a colour which is perhaps best described as salmon-pink. All the examples of this ware which have been noted seem to date c 1805-15, with perhaps a margin of a few years on either side. Moreover, no marked wares of any other manufacturer in quite this colour and treatment are known to the author. Whilst it is dangerous to assert that these attractive wares are unique, it would not be unreasonable to think of Davenport first when making an attribution of an unmarked piece.

The handsome tea service (18) from the City of Liverpool Museum illustrates the shapes of the main vessels and their style of decoration. Two features merit particular comment. The inside of the cups and slop basin, as can be seen, are cream-coloured. Presumably this was thought to be a more attractive background for the tea drinker. The paintings which decorate the whole service are very characteristic. They are in a sepia-toned monochrome, and all are by the same hand. It is most unusual for such a full service in earthenware to have survived. There are four saucers, seven cups and four mugs as well as the larger pieces illustrated. One significant feature is that none of the cups, mugs or saucers is marked, nor is the slop basin, the deep dish or the salt cellar. Thus identification of such items separate from the major pieces would be dependent upon a close comparison of shape, colour (which does vary quite considerably in depth) and decoration. It is perhaps stretching analogy too far to suggest that the factory policy at this period was to mark only the major pieces in services, and possibly the plates, but certainly the caneware pieces mentioned on p 40 also fall into this pattern. Together with this fine Liverpool tea service are ten dessert plates, one of which is shown as (19). These could be part of the tea service, for, though the body is somewhat darker than the teawares, the painting is again by the same hand. It is unusual, however, to find plates of this size as part of a tea service at this period. Significantly, only three of the ten plates are marked. One further plate at Liverpool demands

18 *Coloured body tea service.*
The main pieces from an earthenware tea service. The body of all the wares is coloured a salmon-pink, though the inside of the cups and the slop basin are cream-coloured.
Each piece is enamelled in a sepia-tone monochrome with a rural landscape featuring a building of some kind, a house, a tower, a church etc, with trees and hills in the background. Human figures appear on some, but not all of the pieces. All the paintings appear to have been done by the same hand.
Dimensions:
Slop bowl. Diam 5½in. Height 3½in.
Salt. Height 3¼in.
Teapot. Overall length 11⅜in. Total height 4¾in.
Teapot stand. Length 8½in. Width 7¾in.
Mug. Height 2½in.
Cup. Height 2⅜in.
Saucer. Diam 5¼in.
Cream jug. Overall length 6in. Height 3½in.
Sugar box. Overall length 6½in. Height 4½in.
Mark: No 2 is impressed on the teapot and stand, cream jug, sugar box, but nowhere else (see text).
Date: c 1805-15.
City of Liverpool Museum

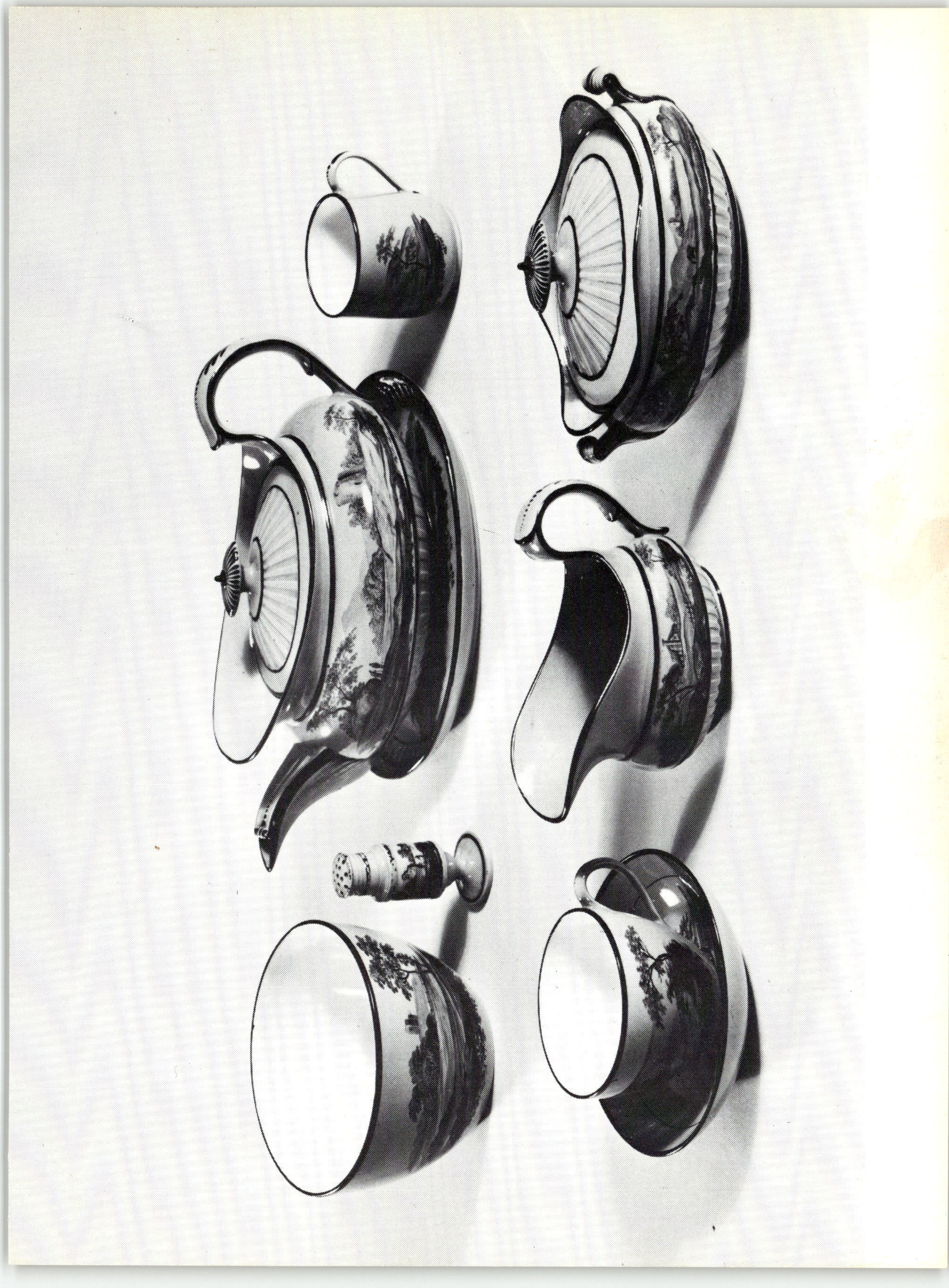

attention. This is *en suite* with the set of ten, but is of a dipped not a stained body. It has a similar monochrome painting, but not by the same hand, and bears the upper case impressed mark and the date numbers for 1856—clearly a replacement, but a most interesting example.

To date only useful wares have been noted in the coloured-body. The pierced dish (20) has rather a different stained body colour from the Liverpool tea service. It is more of a buff colour, but is of the same class of ware. The workmanship is of a high standard, and a full service would be most desirable.

Perhaps the best-known wares in this medium are teapots. An example with a monochrome painting on the body from the Hanley Museum collection has been illustrated in Geoffrey Bemrose, plate 17b, and in Godden's *Encyclopaedia*, plate 193. Godden also illustrates a very fine jug (plate 194) in what he describes as an orange-brown earthenware, again typically decorated with a monochrome landscape. The Hanley teapot has a companion piece similarly decorated in the Victoria and Albert Museum, though of a slightly larger size. Both are of the same 'low Egyptian' type of shape. The pot in (21) is also from Hanley and its black enamel decoration is as attractive as the landscape paintings on the other pieces. All the teapots are marked. None of the pieces bears any kind of pattern mark.

It need hardly be stressed that this most attractive class of ware is extremely rare.

19 *(above left) Coloured-body plate.*
Plate with a strong red-coloured body, decorated with a sepia monochrome painting of a river scene with a three-arch bridge, some ruined buildings, a tree prominent in the right foreground with hills in the background.
Diam 9in. Mark: No 2. Date: c 1810.
City of Liverpool Museum

20 *(above right) Coloured-body pierced dessert dish.*
Buff or deep cream-coloured earthenware dish. It is heart-shaped with an out-turned rim, moulded and pierced in basket form. Decorated at the bottom with four small flower sprigs in crimson and with an 'egg and tongue' border pattern in crimson. The lines at the rim and base are in dull blue.
Width 7¾in. Mark: No 2. Date: c 1800-10.
Victoria and Albert Museum

21 *(below) Coloured-body teapot.*
Salmon-coloured teapot decorated with leaf designs and geometric patterns in black monochrome enamel. The piece has a squat but elongated appearance.
Height 3¾in. Maximum width 8¾in. Mark: No 2. Date: c 1805-15.
Hanley Museum, Stoke-on-Trent

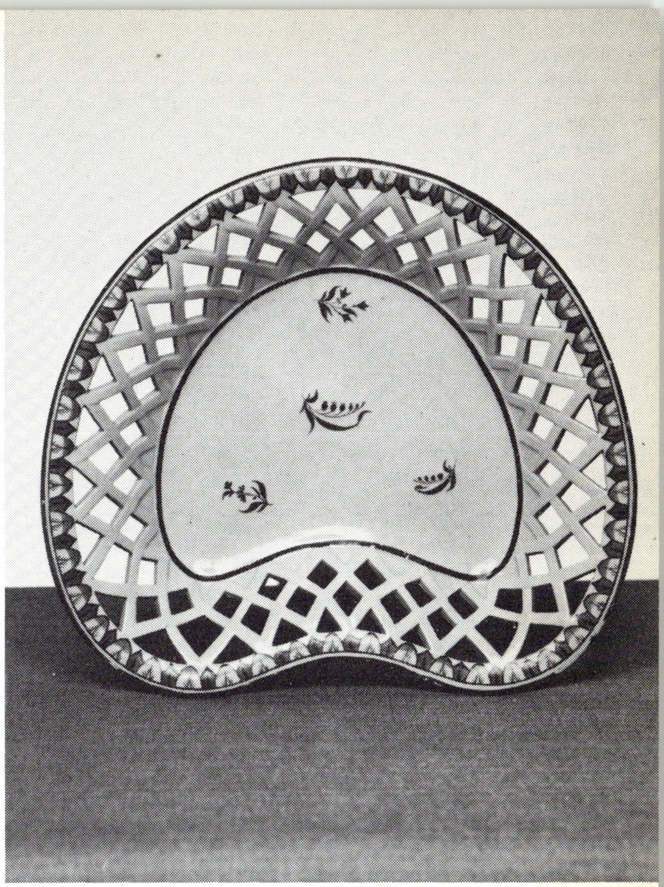

Transfer-Printed Earthenware

The technical process whereby a pattern engraved on to a copper plate is transferred by the medium of an inked tissue paper to the surface of biscuit earthenware, and is then fixed by firing in the 'hardening-on kiln', and subsequently glazed and fired again in the 'glost oven', is detailed in full in A. W. Coysh *Blue and White Transfer Ware*, pp 7-8. For John Davenport and his contemporaries, underglaze printing provided a most effective substitute for hand-painted wares, and the process was well-established in 1794 when Unicorn Bank was purchased.

The earliest Davenport printed pattern would appear to be the *Chinoiserie Bridgeless Pattern*, sometimes erroneously called a *Willow Pattern* (Coysh, plate 27). In order to widen the range, only a few of the patterns published by Mr Coysh have been repeated in this book. Many of those he illustrates are amongst the most popular and frequently encountered, and these will be noted. Mr Coysh has given names to several patterns and for clarity's sake these have been retained, and are indicated thus: (C). Where the present author has invented the pattern name this is indicated as (A). When a pattern name is given without attribution, this is the factory name as printed on the ware. The earliest examples of the above pattern, such as a plate in the author's collection impressed with the anchor alone, could qualify for an eighteenth-century date.

Another early pattern frequently found is the *Chinoiserie Ruins Pattern* (C) (Coysh, plate 26). This may also be found on wares which could be dated to the turn of the century. A pattern which cannot claim that distinction is illustrated here (22). Coysh named it the *Chinese River Scene*, and that will serve. It is, in fact, 'View of the Imperial Park at Gehol' and is taken from John Barrow, *Travels in China*, T. Cadell & W. Davies (publ) 1806, facing p 128. (I am much indebted to Mrs Judith Busby for this information.) It was common practice for the engraver to seek out suitable scenes from prints in travel books, to adapt as transfer-printed patterns. Here is an interesting field of research, for hardly any of the multitude of Davenport printed patterns has been traced to the source.

That difficulty does not arise with the *Willow*

22 *(above left) Blue and white transfer printed plate. Plate printed in dark medium blue with the 'Chinese River Scene' (C) pattern. (See text for derivation.) The border is composed rather incongruously of English flowers, geometrical motifs and dragon-like creatures. There is a very shallow foot rim. The glaze underneath shows considerable blue.*
Diam 9¾in. Mark: No 2. Date: c 1810.

23 *(above right) Blue and white transfer-printed arcaded plate.*
Arcaded plate printed in medium blue with the Willow pattern. The inner rim is moulded in the form of basket work or plaited reeds, the outer rim is pierced. There are sixty-four arcades or pierced holes. No foot rim.
Diam 7in. Mark: No 3. Date: c 1815-25.

24 *(below) Blue and white transfer-printed pierced dessert or vegetable basket.*
Basket printed in medium blue with the 'Tudor Mansion' (C) pattern. In the foreground a man holds a fishing net, a boy holds a rod. The border is composed of branches from two different types of tree. The pierced portion does not reach to the base as on (4). The handles are painted in a scale pattern and have two spurs, one on top, one inside or beneath.
Length (without handles) 10¼in. Width 7in. Height 3in. Mark: No 2. Date: c 1810-20.

Pattern (23) which is not common on Davenport wares, especially those of an early date. The arcaded plate itself is of interest, similar pieces were manufactured at Herculaneum, Liverpool, and by Spode amongst others. There is little point in counting the arcades as the Herculaneum and Spode examples of the same size also have sixty-four arcades!

The basket (24) printed with the *Tudor Mansion Pattern* (C), though pierced, is not of the same form as the creamware piece (4)—the piercing does not reach to the base. Thus although still light in weight, it is more serviceable and not so fragile as the creamware. The border pattern is interesting and distinctive, though a somewhat similar design may be seen on the wares of David Dunderdale from Castleford (see Little, W. L., plate 104). Mr Little also illustrates two interesting Davenport plates. One (Little, plate 23) is a rustic scene with a watermill and two men standing by a horse and cart and is quite rare, the second piece (Little, plate 24) is a plate printed in a peculiar dark blue with a pseudo-classical scene said to have been designed by the engraver William Brookes of Port Vale, Wolstanton. This is very rare and may be seen in the Victoria & Albert Museum.

The pieces illustrated as (25, 26 and 27) all bear fishing scenes which are comparatively rare. All carry the impressed mark No 2, and almost certainly pre-date 1820. They are amongst the most attractive of the patterns, being printed in a soft blue. They have the additional interest of the ruined building as a backcloth to the fishing scenes. The treatment of the trees, of which the right-hand side one droops down into the scene, is very characteristic of at least one of the engravers who worked for Davenport.

Amongst other comparatively early patterns—pre-1830 which are met with fairly frequently—are the *Chinoiserie High Bridge Pattern* (C) (Coysh, plate 30), the *Mosque and Fishermen Pattern* (C) (Coysh, plate 32), *The Villagers* (C) (Coysh, plate 33) and the *Mare and Foal Pattern* (C) (Coysh, plate 34). Most common of all is the *Bamboo and Peony Pattern* (C) (Coysh, plate 29), which may be found on stone china as well as on the ordinary earthenware body. The pattern continued in use certainly until the 1840s. None of these early patterns has a printed factory pattern name. This

The 'Fisherman' series.

25 (above left) Blue and white transfer printed triangular supper dish.

Printed in light medium blue with the 'Fisherman's Tale' (A) pattern. Framed by trees, with a ruined abbey in the background in which two or three figures stand, a fisherman, his arms at full extent, shows a fellow angler 'the one that got away'. Beside him is a basket full of fish; to his right another angler has just cast. Border design an elaborate geometrical pattern. Rippled glaze.

Maximum dimensions $10\frac{1}{2}$in × $7\frac{1}{4}$in. Mark: No 2. Date: c 1810-20.

26 (above right) Blue and white transfer-printed arcaded plate.

Printed in medium blue with the 'Fisherman and Fence' (A) pattern. Framed by trees with a ruined abbey in the background where a man and a woman walk, a fisherman is holding his long 'angle'. He has a creel over his shoulder, behind him is a fence of four posts and cross-piece. The inner rim is of moulded basket-work, the outer rim is pierced with sixty-four arcades painted blue. Rippled glaze. (Damaged). Diam 7in. Mark and date as on (25).

27 (below) Blue and white transfer-printed pierced dessert or vegetable basket and stand.

Left: Stand printed in light medium blue with the 'Solitary Fisherman' (A) pattern. Framed by trees with a ruined cottage and church in the background in which stand two figures, a solitary fisherman is seated holding his rod; to his immediate left is a creel. There is a $\frac{3}{4}$in pierced inner rim and a $\frac{3}{4}$in outer rim printed with an elaborate geometric pattern. Rippled glaze.

Length 10in. Width $7\frac{3}{4}$in. Mark and date as on (25).

Right: Basket (damaged) printed in light medium blue with the 'Fisherman and Friend' (A) pattern. Framed by trees with a ruined church with tower in the background, the seated angler holds his rod whilst his 'friend' stands to his left. Border as on stand. The piece has been riveted and lacks handles. It is more oval in shape than (24).

Length 10in. Width $7\frac{3}{4}$in. Mark and date as on (25).

practice seems to have begun in the 1830s. Most of the earlier pieces are notably light in weight, and though marking prior to 1820 is somewhat erratic, the frequency of marks after that date is high.

During the 1830s changes took place in the production of transfer-printed wares. The traditional blue was becoming old-fashioned, the chinoiserie scenes out of date (though never entirely discarded). Printing in colours other than blue had already been introduced, and now black, green, pink, grey and brown prints, all were fashionable. Even the blue printing changed and fashion demanded either a very pale blue such as we see on (29), or the aesthetically offensive 'flown blue' (33). These general changes are mirrored on Davenport wares. The blue tones soften (or weaken), the scenes become more delicate, less bold and certainly less striking. Good examples of this trend can be seen in (29, 30 and 32) which are printed in comparatively pale shades. The engraving on (29) is beautifully subtle and fine, whilst that on (32) is sketchy and because of the pale colour much less satisfying than that seen on earlier wares. The shapes of (30 and 32) should also be noted. The jug (31) is printed in a good firm blue, but the design is both heavily detailed and poorly defined. The great interest of this piece is the very rare mark No 5 which dates it to the period of a partnership between Henry and William Davenport.

It could be of just such a pot that John Davenport wrote on 19 July 1834 (*Foxley* 73). The letter contains a most concise description of what to look for in a good blue printed pot:

Dear Henry,

I have been here all day engaged with our Travellers, on the subject of prices & patterns—that is new patterns of Blue Table Ware in which we are behind Mintons & Ridgways—What is wanting is the exercise of more Judgment in the selection of Patterns—we have been very successful in two lately viz the Rhenish Views, & the *Leaf Border*—and I am anxious to have something very good now fixed upon—It must be particularly studied in the Border in which much of the effect lays—White brought some Swiss Scenery wch I send you, but it is too much like the last. On looking over much of the Ware, I must remark that a good deal of it is very

28 *(above left) Blue and white transfer-printed child's chamber pot.*
Printed in dark medium blue with the 'Muleteer' pattern. A man rides a mule attended by three others. In the right background are a group of houses and two churches; to the left a waterfall, fence and a river with further buildings on the bank.
Diam 5½in. Mark: No 8 printed in blue with the pattern name MULETEER in a small cartouche. Date: c 1830-40.

Mr and Mrs J. K. des Fontaines

29 *(above right) Blue and white transfer-printed plate with gilding.*
Printed in pale blue with the 'Swiss Fishing Scene' (A) pattern. Framed by two silver birch trees are two fishermen in a punt. One is 'poling', the other is hauling in a fishing net. They are on a lake with a Swiss village in the background with a sweep of mountain behind. A dotted gilt pattern frames the well of the plate. The rim is printed with a design of densely packed wavy lines bounded by a twisted rope outlined in gilt.
Diam 10½in. Mark: DAVENPORT printed in blue and No 3 impressed, with '5' also impressed above the name. Date: 1835-40.

30 *(below) Blue and white transfer-printed teapot.*
Printed in light blue with the 'Chinese Garden Scene' (A) pattern. Two Chinese figures converse in front of a single-storey house. In the centre is a flowering tree and beneath it to the left a large bowl of flowers. A small tower is in the background with hills in the distance. The rim is decorated with English flowers in 'C' scrolls embellished with geometric patterns; likewise the lid.
Length 9½in. Max height 5¼in. Mark: No 3 printed in blue in a large size. Date: c 1830-50 (see text).

Hanley Museum, Stoke-on-Trent

roughly got up by the Workmen in the Clay—badly printed with soft Oils, & badly laid on by the Transferrers—a good deal dirtied in the Glaze Tub in dipping—some much *run* together in the Blue, as *I presume* by being placed *wet*, or not properly dried before putting into the Hardening Kiln—the cockspur marks are very bad, & I think what you make *now* at Longport must be bung, as I believe Spodes & Mintons are. I have sent you down a China jar as the best way of explaining its defects—You will see how badly it is got up in the Clay from the Molds (sic)—no Sharpness—seams not rubbed down—no lining round the ornaments with a Tool—the Handles hardly stuck on at all—and sent *from Biscuit W'house* without stopping the Spouts &c &c—the Blue badly laid on. But indeed ought such a piece to have been Ornamented in that expensive manner, if at all . . .

The 'flown blue' piece (33) illustrates how the printed design instead of remaining sharp is encouraged to spread or fuse into the glaze producing a deliberately blurred effect. It is said to have been produced by firing the ware in an atmosphere containing volatile chlorides. A great quantity of ware was made in this finish which was most popular in the period 1840-70. In the letter from John Wardle to John Lockett quoted on p 24, Wardle when writing of the Indian market says 'also H'hd of dinner ware same quantity are sent of flowing blue *NOT* landscape pattn's, these are objected to'. Modern taste objects to flowing blue—but then times change!

The plate (34) is an example of printing in a colour other than blue. This grey print of the *Montilla* pattern probably dates from the late 1850s, though the piece illustrated here has date numbers for 1865. The border pattern, like that on the *Friburg* tea pot (31) is very typical of the 1850s and 60s.

There is no certainty that any of the Davenport patterns were engraved in the factory. Specialist firms of engravers existed to cater for the needs of the potter, and it is possible that all the many different patterns produced were done by outside engravers. Apart from Brookes mentioned earlier, one other name is associated with the firm—James Cutts of Snow Hill, Shelton. He worked in Staffordshire from c 1834-70. A number of his designs exist as 'pulls' from the original

31 *(above left) Blue and white transfer-printed jug.*
Printed in medium blue with the 'Statuary' pattern. A garden scene with buildings in the distance is the setting for a figure of a woman pouring water from a pitcher into an urn beside her. The border consists of flowers and an elaborate geometrical pattern.
Height 6¼in. Mark: No 3 impressed and No 5 printed. Date: 1832-5.

32 *(above right) Blue and white transfer-printed hexagonal teapot.*
Printed in very pale blue with the 'Friburg' pattern. A 'Gothic' building is prominent on the right, with a tree on the left, and a further house on the riverbank in the distance. The border is a design of a meandering garland of flowers encircling panels which alternately contain a rose spray. The whole rests upon concentric circular lines. The spout is hexagonal in section. The handle large and squarish in outline.
Overall height 9in. Mark: No 8 printed in blue; also a crown surmounting a garter upon which is printed IRONSTONE and within FRIBURG. Date: 1850-60.

33 *(below left) 'Flown' blue and white transfer-printed plate.*
Printed in dark flown blue with the 'Amoy' pattern. In a garden two Chinese ladies shelter under a parasol. Printed flower groups and geometric designs decorate the rim. There is a very considerable amount of blue in the glaze, especially on the back.
Diam 10½in. Mark: No 4 with the date numbers '4 4' impressed. Printed in an oblong cartouche the pattern name AMOY. Date: 1844.

34 *(below right) Grey and white transfer-printed plate.*
Printed in grey with the 'Montilla' pattern. To the right is a pseudo-Gothic temple in the doorway of which a woman is standing. On the left foreground stands a tree. There are further buildings in the background. The border consists of concentric circular lines upon which are placed flower sprays and scrolls.
Diam 9in. Mark: No 8 printed in grey with an elaborate pattern mark—the word IRONSTONE over an eagle perched on a branch, and on a ribbon the name MONTILLA. Also No 12, impressed with date numbers '8:65'. Date: August 1865.

copper plates and are to be found in the Victoria & Albert Museum print collection. His scenes are rather romantic and ethereal. His work is occasionally signed. (Mankowitz and Haggar, p 63 illustrate a backstamp mark signed by Cutts.) It has not been possible in a work of this scope to attempt to list and describe the Davenport designs for which Cutts was responsible.

Another aspect of printing in colours other than blue can be seen on (35 and 36). The latter with its fascinating collection of marks has a blue centre and a green border—a most unusual combination on earthenware. Geoffrey Godden in his *Encyclopaedia*, colour plate V, depicts a multi-colour service of Davenport earthenware, and in the Liverpool Museum collection a plate with the same scene as (29) is printed in three colours—blue, black and green. This piece has date numbers for 1836 which is the same date as the *Waverley* piece. In the Victoria and Albert Museum a companion Scott piece, *The Legend of Montrose*, is printed in pink. Geoffrey Godden in *Collector's Guide* (November 1971, p 75) speculates that Jesse Austin, the designer and engraver of Pratt 'pot lid' fame, may have been concerned in experiments in multi-colour printing at Davenports in the 1830s. This is an interesting theory for which confirmatory evidence may yet be found.

It is clear that the *Waverley* plate was made for export to America. It is equally obvious that (35), the *British America* plate, was destined for Canada. Mrs Elizabeth Collard in her fine book devotes a chapter to 'Davenport and Canada'. She deals in considerable detail with this most interesting plate which is printed in pink. The *British America* was built in 1829 and was a familiar sight on the St Lawrence at Montreal, the view of which may well have been adapted from a set of views of the city by Robert A. Sproule published in 1830 (see Elizabeth Collard, pp 239-245).

The plate in (37) with its armorial design enlarged in (38) was for a rather different market. This Russian plate is something of a puzzle. It is of a similar moulded form to the porcelain plate (76) without the piercings which, however, can be seen in the moulding. It is only of moderate quality. The armorial has not been traced, though the crest of the double-headed eagle is normally associated with the Romanovs. The piece just does not seem good enough for the nobility—unless it

35 *(above left) Pink and white transfer-printed plate. Printed in pink with a view of Montreal seen from St Helen's Island, and depicting the St Lawrence steamboat 'British America'.*
Diam 10in. Mark: No 3 and the printed pattern name MONTREAL. Date: c 1832-40.
Elizabeth Collard, Montreal

36 *(above right) Green, blue and white transfer-printed plate.*
Printed in pale green on the rim with a broad design of wild flowers and a scroll and dentil pattern. In the centre printed in blue with a scene from the novel 'Waverley' by Sir Walter Scott.
Diam 9¾in. Marks: No 6 printed in blue, No 7 printed in green and No 4 impressed with date numbers '3 6'. Date: 1836.

37 *(below left) Blue and white transfer-printed plate. Printed in medium blue with an armorial crest. The well of the plate outlined with blue as is the rim with the addition of gilding. The moulding of the rim is the same as that on the pierced plate (76).*
Diam 9½in. Mark: No 4 with date numbers '5 2' and DAVENPORT printed in blue, and the legend printed as in (39). Date: 1852.

38 *(below right) Close-up of the armorial on (37). The crest is surmounted by a double-headed eagle. The motto may be translated, 'Glory to God and Life to Thee'.*

39 *(bottom right) Mark on Russian armorial plate, printed in blue on the back of the plate in large letters. The mark measures 1⅛in × ⅜in and may be translated as STORM or TEMPEST.*

БУР Я

was for use by the servants! Its appearance is very suggestive of ship's crockery or hotel ware.

Finally, in connection with exports, it is probably true to say that as much printed ware found its way abroad as was sold in Britain. The Davenports were predominantly a firm of exporters. An indication of what might be found abroad is given by the unique drug jars (40 and 41). These are part of a remarkable series of twenty-six syrup jars, twenty-two small, seventeen medium and two large jars for other medical preparations which were purchased for the Wellcome collection in 1910 from a Venetian pharmacy. (For further details see J. K. Crellin, p 122.) Though no other drug jars are known, there is plenty of scope for the collector of unusual and quasi-medical items. The charming, child's chamber pot (28) printed with the *Muleteer Pattern* would make an excellent beginning, to which could be added other items noted in the Wellcome collection and elsewhere. Such wares would include feeding cups (42) and food warmers (43), pap boats, commode buckets, urinal flasks and bordalous, as well as footbaths and all the accessories which were produced with bedroom toilet sets. All had their place in the repertoire of Davenport printed wares.

It is manifestly impossible to compile a check list of items made or patterns printed for such a large factory which lasted for nearly a century. Tea wares, dinner and dessert wares, toilet wares, decorative items—Davenport made them all.

40 *(above left) Grey and white transfer-printed drug jar and cover.*
Printed in grey with the 'Durham' pattern. In the foreground a man is fishing attended by a lady and child, in the background is a view of the city with the bridge and cathedral prominent. The border is floral with stippling and a scrollwork design. The handles are modelled as rams' heads, picked out in pink lustre. The cover finial is likewise touched with lustre.
Height 12in. Mark: No 8 printed in black with the pattern name DURHAM. Date: c 1850-60.
Wellcome Institute of the History of Medicine

41 *(above right) Grey and white transfer-printed syrup jar and cover.*
Printed in grey with the 'Durham' pattern as above. Strap handle.
Height 15in. Mark and date as on (40).
Wellcome Institute of the History of Medicine

42 *(below left) Blue and white transfer-printed invalid feeding cup.*
Printed in blue with a scene in which a cathedral or church dominates the background whilst a single-span bridge is in the foreground. The border printed with flowers, a bird on a twig and a series of lines and dentil shapes. The handle is double-ribbed and is set at right angles to the spout.
Height 3in. Diam $4\frac{1}{2}$in. Mark: No 8 printed with an indecipherable pattern name. Date: c 1850-60.
Wellcome Institute of the History of Medicine

43 *(below right) Blue and white transfer-printed food warmer.*
Printed in medium blue with a meandering floral pattern. The body of the vessel is pierced by numerous round holes and four heart-shaped ones. The handles are slightly scrolled and the opening is straight-sided with a curved arch. There is no top.
Height $6\frac{1}{2}$in. Diam $5\frac{1}{2}$in (without handles). Mark: No 8 printed in blue with no pattern name. Date: c 1850-60.
Wellcome Institute of the History of Medicine

Stone China

The origin of stone china is not entirely clear. In 1800, John and William Turner took out a patent for a new fabric, in fact a stone china, which is termed Turner's Patent. In 1805-06, the brothers went bankrupt and production of stone china ceased. It has always been asserted that Spode took over the patent and made the ware subsequently. (Geoffrey Godden, *Masons*, p 7 and p 92, seems partially to accept this view.) But, according to Leonard Whiter, this was not so. In an excellent analysis of the evidence, he strongly indicates that Spode did not make stone china until after 1813 (*Spode*, pp 188-192). It seems odd that this very successful and durable ware should have been allowed to lapse, and Reginald Haggar has convincingly suggested that Miles Mason was manufacturing stone china in the period 1806-13, at which date he retired to Liverpool leaving his sons Charles James and George Miles in possession. It was in 1813 that they patented the famous 'Mason's Patent Ironstone China'.

Following Mason's Patent, Spode certainly entered the market, as did other potters including John Davenport. The exact date of manufacture is not known, but it was well-established by 1818 as the letter (*Foxley* 2) already quoted on p 11 indicates. There is an interesting addition:

> We succeeded in competing for the sale of two Dinner Services by the superior appearance of your No 6, which we hope will not be allowed to fall off in whiteness, which is a great object.
>
> We are of opinion that it would be a politic measure to change the Name of it to 'Metallic Porcelain' as we must now Cry down the Ironstone, *at least the Patent* and it will warrant any one to do so as in fact it is now *bad earthenware* . . . Say what you think of changing the name of the Stone ware and inform us the price of Breakfast and Tea ware No 6 and the Brosely Pattern.

On the cover is written, 'Davenports Improved Ironstone' and 'Davenports Improved Metallic Porcelain', both are scored through, and so the ware retained the name stone china.

The pattern 6 quoted may well be that depicted in (44). The piece exemplifies many of the characteristics associated with stone china. It is

44 *(above left) Stone china jug.*
Small jug printed in underglaze blue with an Imari-type pattern of trailing branches, leaves, flowers and an exotic bird. Enamelled overglaze with red, green, pink and yellow, and outlines in gilt.
Height 4½in. Mark: No 9 printed underglaze in blue. No pattern number, but this is stone china pattern number 6. Date: c 1815-20.

45 *(above right) Stone china sauce tureen and cover.*
Printed underglaze with blue outlines, also painted underglaze with 'oven' blue in an Imari-type pattern. Enamelled overglaze in red and green. Gilding at rims and on the handles which are slightly ribbed on the upper side.
Height 5½in. Diam 6½in. Mark: No 9 printed underglaze in blue. Pattern number 37. Date: c 1815-20.

46 *(below) Set of four stone china jugs.*
Octagonal jugs brightly decorated with an underglaze blue printed outline, underglaze painted 'oven' blue and overglaze enamel decoration in red, blue and green, with many touches of gilding. The snake handles are in red with the head and the centre line in green.
Heights (left to right) 4½in, 7in, 5½in, 3½in. Marks: All No 9 printed underglaze in blue. No pattern numbers. Date: c 1820-30.

hard and durable, it does not chip easily and the body has a distinctly greyish hue. It is decorated in an underglaze 'oven' (dark) blue with rather sketchy underglaze blue outlines which serve as a guide to the painting of bright overglaze enamels in shades of pink, orange, red, yellow and green. This pattern 6 is identical with one of Masons (see Godden, *Masons*, plate 98) and with one attributed to Hicks, Meigh & Johnson (see Godden, plate 115; and plate 109 for shapes from a Davenport dessert service in this pattern).

The most popular decorations on stone china were the Imari or Japan patterns, well-exemplified by (45) and by the brash but handsome plates (47 and 48).

A further reminder of the keen competition with Masons is provided by the jugs in (46). These are fine examples of the octagonal jug with snake handle. The difference between the Davenport and the Mason jug is that generally the Davenport piece is better turned-out, neater and crisper in the potting and finish. A very wide variety of ware was made, but again Davenport concentrated on table wares, and we do not find the chimney pieces, garden seats, the huge vases and other fantasies such as C. J. Mason produced. A pattern book distinct from the creamware existed for stone china. The lowest recorded number is pattern 6, the highest a plate with the Broseley pattern printed in blue with gilt embellishments is 142—almost certainly this is not the upper limit.

The two plates (49) are of especial interest, as the one on the right is an early piece c 1820. Its companion, which lacks the three ducks on the border and the stork in the centre, is 'opaque china' and is dated May 1867. A fifty-year life span for a pattern is a potter's dream come true. This latter piece serves as a reminder that even stone china which was such a serviceable body had a limited life. After the mid-1840s it is doubtful if Davenport made any true stone china. The composition of the body changed, and a ware was produced of less-distinctive quality which was called 'opaque china'. A selection of stone china marks is shown on p 111.

47 *(above left) Stone china soup dish.*
Decorated with underglaze dark 'oven' blue, overglaze enamelled brightly on the rim with three panels in red touched with gilding, and in the centre with an oriental flower group in shades of green and red. The two large flowers have delicately painted pink stamens. The body is very clean and white.
Diam 10¼in. Mark: No 11 printed overglaze. Pattern number 58. Date: c 1820-30.

48 *(above right) Stone china plate.*
Decorated with dark underglaze 'oven' blue painted in three panels and several leaves, and enamelled overglaze with patterns of flowers, fences and leaves in red, pink, orange and green. A gilt band decorates the rim; there are touches of gilt on the flowers and there is a central gilt motif.
Diam 10¼in. Mark: No 9 printed overglaze in red. Pattern number 50. Date: c 1820-30.

49 *(below) Opaque china oval dish and stone china plate.*
Right: The plate is decorated with an underglaze blue chinoiserie print and underglaze painted 'oven' blue, depicting a tree, flowers and a stork perched on one leg on the fence. On the border groups of flowers alternate with three cameos of ducks. Enamelled overglaze in pink, orange and green with gilt outlines.
Diam 8in. Mark: No 9 printed underglaze in blue. Pattern number 24. Date: c 1820.
Left: Oval dish decorated with the same pattern as the above but without the duck cameos or the stork on the fence. The colours and gilding are similar though duller and less lively.
Length 10½in. Width 9in. Mark: No 12 and also impressed the date numbers '5:67'. Date: May 1867.

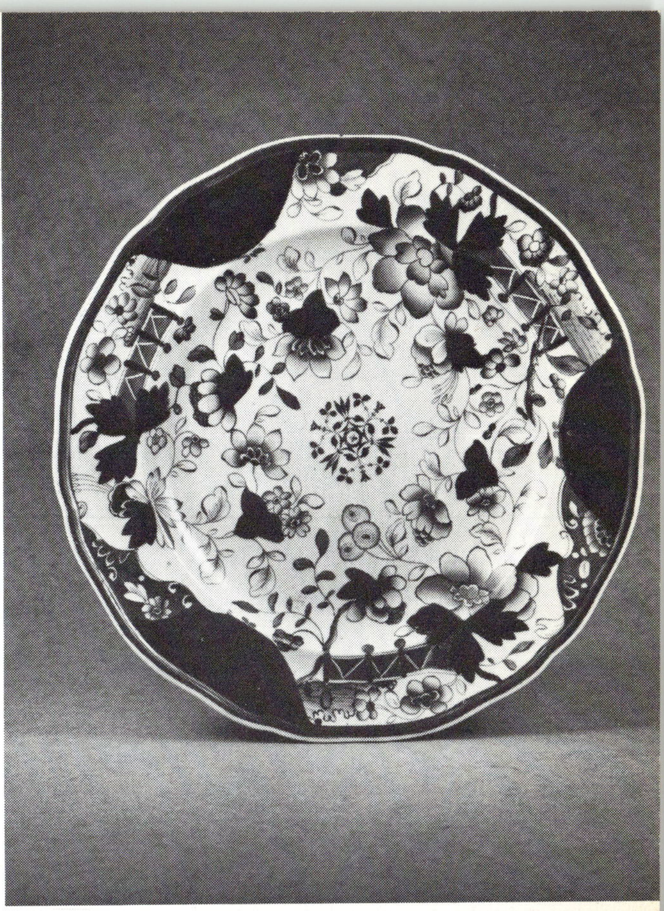

Miscellaneous Earthenwares

There remains an enormous range of earthenwares still to be surveyed in this last section. Yet when one studies the wares closely, there seems little to hold the attention for long. The factory from the 1840s onwards continued to make high-class porcelain wares, but the earthenwares are almost exclusively of a very utilitarian nature. One looks in vain for the coloured majolica glazes such as emanated from Mintons. There are no flights of fantasy into the world of 'Revivals'; no Henri Deux ware; no imitation faience; no mock-Renaissance pieces; not even a really convincing Gothic jug seems to have been produced at Longport. Thus the later earthenwares lack the aesthetic excitement and challenge presented by Worcester, Mintons, Doultons and many contemporary potters. It is perhaps not too harsh to say that the vast majority of Davenport earthenware from c 1840 onwards was crockery.

The illustrations show a small representative sample of these wares. The Toby jug (50) is relatively early, being date-marked for 1836. Compared with the fine coloured-glaze models of the elder Ralph Wood, the Davenport enamelled model is outclassed, but the piece is rare as a collectors' item and more handsome than many of those produced contemporaneously. The plate (51) is also not very common. The fashion for moulded green-glazed ware revived again in the 1840s and 1850s and Wedgwood, Ridgway and others responded. The set of wares (52) is rather more interesting. Probably dating from the 1830s, these are 'chalk body' ware. This type of ware attempted to emulate the lightness in weight of the old creamware, but to be completely white in finish. Victor Pontigny writing to Henry Davenport in 1835 says, 'I have been trying to persuade the folks at Genoa that we are now making CC (cream-coloured) quite equal to Wedgwood & have obtained a trial—see order herewith—pray let it be very white and *light* & well made' (*Foxley* 74). Certainly, the ware is white, light, wellmade and decorated sparingly and most attractively.

The pots depicted in (53, 54 and 55) remind us that Davenports produced more of these miniature pieces than most firms. In no case is the finish particularly good. It is not poor, but one is not drawn to admiration by the delicacy of the potting.

50 *(above left) Earthenware Toby jug.*
Decorated with on-glaze enamel colours. The tricorn hat and the coat are black, the hair grey; the face is flesh-tinted, the cuffs are crimson and the breeches mustard-coloured, giving way below the knees to red and green striped white leggings. The boots are black and the base is sponged a mottled green and red. The foaming tankard is decorated with a large stylised flower. By the right leg rests a pipe.
Height 9½in. Mark: No 4 with the date numbers '3 6' impressed. Date: 1836.
Mr and Mrs D. W. Crompton

51 *(above right) Earthenware green-glazed moulded plate.*
The plate is moulded near the rim with basket-work, the remainder in the form of overlapping leaves. The entire surface is covered in a green glaze which deepens in shade in the recessed portions.
Diam 7¼in. Mark: No 3. Date: c 1850-60.

52 *(below) Group of chalk-body wares.*
Left: Trumpet-shaped spill vase or match pot with down-turned rim in a light, and bright white earthenware, decorated overall in a meandering pattern of pink fronds and green (trefoil) leaves.
Height 4in. Diam at lip 3¾in. Mark: No 3. Date: c 1830-40.
Centre: Kidney-shaped dish with moulded gadroon border and small handle moulded as a leaf and shell. Of the same chalk-body and similarly decorated as the spill vase.
Length 10in. Max width 7¾in. Mark: No 3 impressed and the numbers '36' next to the name. Date: probably 1836.
Right: Octagonal jug with snake handle. Body and decoration as above.
Height 4½in. Mark: No 3. Date: c 1830-40.

The best turned-out piece is the small cup and saucer on the right of (53). It is the earliest piece and has the date numbers for 1836 and bears pattern number 376. This piece, and other earthenware patterns noted, lead to the tentative conclusion that the patterns on ordinary earthenware (unlike the stone china) continued in sequence from the old creamware pattern book.

The child's plate with the printed name EDWARD has the engraving of the name of a good quality, whereas the enamelling is simply paint dabbed on to the ware. Also of interest on (53) is the jelly mould which is of a positive cream colour. It is surprising to find the date numbers for April 1864, one would have placed it much earlier had it not been so dated. Other forms of cream-coloured wares for domestic use were also made at this date.

The variety of shapes depicted in (54) reminds us of what a full dinner service consisted in the mid-nineteenth century. One such blue printed service (full size not miniature) was detailed by John Wardle in the previously quoted letter of 1848 to John Lockett:

1 HHD OF EARTHENWARE ALL OF LIGHT BLUE PD WARE OR 1 TABLE SERVICE COMPLETE
12 DOZ FLAT PLATES 4/-
12 DOZ SOUP DO 4/-
8 DOZ TWIFFLERS 3/6
6 DOZ MUFFINS 6in 3/-
24 HOT WATER PLATES & STOPPERS 1/6
2 ROOT DISHES 6/-
4 COVER DISHES 3/-

18 DISHES	4	4	4	2	2	1	1	(quantity)
	9	10	12	14	16	18	20	(size)
	9d	1/-	1/6	2/6	3/6	4/6	5/6EA.	(cost)

18 20 In
2 GRAVY DISHES 6/6 7/6 EA
1 1
2 BAKERS 10 11 In
1/6 1/9 EA
2 SOUP TUREENS COMPT 11 10/6 EA
2 SAUCE Do „ 3/- „
2 SALADS 3/- „
2 BOATS AND STANDS 1/- „

It was on the mass-production of huge quantities of tablewares of this kind that Davenports concentrated in these later years.

Of the wares shown in (55) special attention may

53 *(above) Group of dated miniature earthenwares.*
Left: Small cup and saucer transfer printed underglaze in black with a geometric design.
Saucer diam $4\frac{3}{4}$in. Cup height 2in. Mark: No 4 with date numbers '5 2' impressed. Date: 1852.
Centre: Child's plate in white earthenware with roughly moulded floral motifs on the rim, coloured crudely in blue, orange and red overglaze enamels. In the centre, EDWARD is printed overglaze in pink in an elaborate cartouche.
Diam $5\frac{1}{2}$in. Mark: No 4 with date numbers '3 5' impressed. Date: 1835.
Miniature jelly mould in pale cream-coloured earthenware.
Length $2\frac{3}{8}$in. Width $2\frac{1}{2}$in. Height $1\frac{1}{2}$in. Mark: No 3 with date numbers '4:64' impressed. Date: April 1864.
Right: Miniature cup and saucer in white earthenware. Attractively enamelled in red, black and yellow with flower groups.
Saucer diam 4in. Cup height $1\frac{1}{2}$in. Mark: No 4 with date numbers '3 6' impressed. Pattern number 376. Date: 1836.

54 *(below) Group of wares forming part of a miniature or 'doll's' earthenware dinner service.*
The decoration is transfer-printed underglaze in a light medium blue. It consists of an all-over stylised floral pattern.
The service consists of three sizes of flat plate, soup plates, four meat dishes in graduated sizes, two soup tureens and stands and two covered vegetable dishes. Mark: (on all but about two of the pieces) No 3. Date: c 1840-50.

Elizabeth Collard, Montreal

EDWARD

be drawn to the lustre wares of pattern 701 (pieces with lustre decoration and pattern 702 have also been noted). This pattern number served for porcelain decoration also (see 84 iv). As many of the lustre wares are unmarked a clear knowledge of this pattern is an aid to authentication. A remarkable example of Davenport lustre ware is the immense silver lustre jug in the City of Liverpool Museum. The piece is 25in high, has an overall width of 29in and a maximum circumference of 65½in. Upon it is an inscription 'Eyo Archibong Esquire'. It is impressed with mark No 3. A museum card within the jug reads, 'Silver lustre jug, manufactured by Davenport for an African chief Eyo Archibong, Calabar. This is one of a dozen made to the order of the Chief to store rum.' The jug was presented to the Museum in 1912. Any firm capable of producing silver lustre ware on this grand scale must have used lustres in other ways than simply to ornament miniature tea wares. One must suspect that a quantity of unmarked lustre was produced at Davenports. Certainly in the later years a nacreous, mother-of-pearl type lustre was used over a coloured printed decoration. This has been noted in conjunction with several patterns, including *Ceres* and *Ivy Wreaths*. A wash of pink lustre all over the glaze on printed wares has also been observed, mainly on jugs and mugs of the 1850-60 period.

The handsome pie dish (56) brings us back to the kitchen for which so many wares were made. Mrs Elizabeth Collard (op cit plate 8) illustrates a moulded bread tray in opaque china, and the author has a soap dish and large wash bowl, both competently enamelled with flowers, part of an opaque china toilet set of which countless thousands must have been made in the 1860s and 1870s.

One further type of ware demands specific attention. This is a class of articles having a matt black-painted surface upon which are enamelled flower groups in bright colours. An interesting small collection of these wares is in the Weston Park Museum, Sheffield. Amongst them are a tea pot and coffee pot, a plate, a pair of candlesticks and a pair of match pots (spill vases). All are marked and the plate has date numbers for 1856. Other items of tableware have been noted in this unusual and quite attractive black and coloured ware.

The last three illustrations in this section (57, 58 and 59) depict earthenware printed patterns

55 *(above) Miscellaneous and miniature earthenwares.*

Top: Miniature teapot and sucrier, transfer-printed underglaze in grey-green with a Maltese cross pattern. Teapot height 4in, length 6in. Sucrier height 3¼in, length 3¾in. Marks: Both have DAVENPORT printed and impressed marks—probably No 4—too blurred to read. (A miniature plate, cup and saucer with the same pattern in blue bear date letters for 1844.) Date: c 1840-55.

Bottom: Miniature teapot and saucer in opaque china. Both decorated with large blooms in pink lustre, and with bands of lustre at the rims, with fronds, sparse leaves and small flowers in green and red enamel.

Teapot height 4in, overall length 6in. Saucer diam 4½in. Marks: Both have pattern number 701. The teapot has an impressed mark—probably No 4—too blurred to read. The saucer has No 12 with date numbers '6 0'. Date: Saucer 1860. Teapot c 1845-60. See also (84).

Cup and saucer transfer printed underglaze in deep flown blue with floral motifs and trophies. Touched overglaze with red enamel.

Saucer diam 5¾in. Cup height 2¼in. Marks: printed DAVENPORT, a pseudo-Chinese seal mark and the pattern name NANKIN. Painted pattern number 717, and No 4 mark impressed with date numbers '4 4'. Date: 1844.

56 *(below) Earthenware pie dish.*

Large covered pie dish in cane-coloured earthenware, elaborately moulded in the form of decorated pastry crust with moulded finial in vegetable form (slightly damaged). Fully glazed outside and within.

Length 10½in. Width 8½in. Height 5¼in. Mark: No 3 with impressed date numbers '7:64'. Date: July 1864.

on simple unsophisticated wares which ought to be within the means of any collector. They are mass-produced articles, cheap even when made, and the finish to the jug (59) would have annoyed John Davenport beyond measure. They have been included, as indeed have many other of the pots in this section for the sake of completeness. They represent a departure from the tradition of blue printing, in that the printed part of the pattern is incomplete without touches of overglaze enamel. The Japanese-style plate (58) is a reminder of the influence of the Aesthetic movement in the 1870s and 1880s. It is printed throughout in colours and possesses a curious period attraction, as indeed so has the printed pattern *Oceana* in which a printed crab has a prominent place in the design! A jug of the same pattern as (57) in the York Castle Museum collection has the pattern name *Royal Chints* upon it.

When the factory closed in 1887 some of the copper plates for printing were purchased by A. Wenger of Hanley who in a supplement to the *Pottery Gazette*, 1 February 1888 advertised a willingness to 'sell or hire and to match the colours and supply the shapes used with the following patterns'. The full list is reprinted below. Some of these patterns are well-known and most of them seem to date from the period 1850-80.

Montilla, Athens, Bramble, Garland, Pastoral, Scots, Alpine Amusements, Lily, Crosslet, Fan, Old Florida, Nile, Eastern Bird, Rocailles, Citron, Grapes, Whampoa, Danish, Iolanthe, Syrian, Ceres, Chinese Scenery, Cyprus, Woodland, Park, Ribbon, Arabesque, Bird and Berry, Canton, Versailles, Spanish Rose, Gothic, Sunflower, Tendril, Swallow and Nightshade, Fish, Italian, Honeysuckle, Bird and Star, Muleteer, Genoa, Hop, Nectarine, Madras, French Fan, Delaware, British Scenery, Pekin, Flora, Festoon and Bird, Fishermen, Asiatic Pheasant, Squirrel, Marbles.

It is likely that the patterns listed above represent only a proportion of printed patterns used by the firm over its last thirty years or so. Here is plenty of scope for the collector, both to identify the listed patterns and discover new ones.

57 *(above left) Green transfer-printed and enamelled plate.*
Printed in green with the 'Royal Chints' (sic) pattern in an all-over design of fronds and a background of stippling. The overglaze enamel decoration is of stylised flowers in pink and harebells in blue.
Diam 8¾in. Mark: No 3. No pattern name or number. Date: c 1835-50.

58 *(above right) Colour-printed earthenware plate.*
Scalloped edge plate decorated with a Japanese-style print in several colours. The main motifs are a flower pot and blossom, a fan decorated with a view of a junk, and two groups of flowers and a stork. Not marked as such, but this is the 'Fan' pattern (see p 70). Diam 10in. Marks: DAVENPORT printed in black, design registration impressed (see mark No 20) for 1879. No 3 and impressed date numbers '10:79'. Date: October 1879.

59 *(below left) Printed and enamelled earthenware jug.*
Small jug transfer-printed in black with the 'Whampoa' pattern and enamelled overglaze with crude splashes of green and blue.
Height 5in. Marks: A printed floral cartouche (see No 8) with pattern name WHAMPOA and DAVENPORT. Pattern number 854. Date: c 1860-75.

60 *(below right) John Davenport.*
Bust portrait taken from an engraving signed, 'Yours sincerely J'n Davenport' and 'John Philip RA pinx, W. H. Mote sculp.' Published as the frontispiece to Sleigh, John, A History of the Ancient Parish of Leek in Staffordshire *(1883).*

Porcelain

DESSERT WARES

The exact date when John Davenport began to manufacture porcelain is not known. A statement that he 'had made a trip to France prior to 1800 to study the French methods of making porcelain, with the result that he produced a body superior to anything then made in England', occurs in G. W. and F. A. Rhead, p 282, and has frequently been repeated subsequently. But as Simeon Shaw, Ward and Jewitt make no mention of such a visit and as England and France were at war 1793-1802, such a visit is unlikely. This story may well have arisen as a consequence of the report on the Royal visit of 1806 (see p 10). The Prince was shown refined porcelain products in the French taste ('equal to the old Seve'). What is clear from HRH's visit is that Davenport porcelain was not experimental. It was a bone china of the type developed and marketed by Josiah Spode towards the end of the 1790s (see L. Whiter, pp 24-30 for a balanced discussion of the development of bone china). It became the basic paste of all the Staffordshire porcelain-making factories. Bone china consisted of 25-50 per cent of calcined ox bones mixed with china clay and china stone in roughly equal proportions, and on occasions with flint and blue clay also added. Probably therefore at about the turn of the century John Davenport began to produce a fine-quality bone china, decorated and styled in the French manner.

The earliest known Davenport porcelains are those marked with the word 'Longport' in red script (No 13, last plate). Two such pieces are illustrated here (61 and 63). They are of a good body with a fairly thick glaze which has crazed and in consequence they have become slightly yellowed in a manner similar to wares from Bloor's Derby and to some early Rockingham pieces. The scenic plate is one of four similar known to the author, all painted by the same hand. On style alone it does not seem realistic to date these pieces much earlier than 1805. Nor can any other 'Longport' signed pieces be attributed to a significantly earlier date. It may well be that the earliest porcelains were quite unmarked. This point is considered in more detail on p 86 and p 98. None of these 'Longport' pieces carried a pattern number.

61 *(above left) Porcelain plate.*
Dessert plate decorated with an enamel painting of a small country house (not identified) backed by hills, with a tree prominent in the right foreground. Gilding on the rim.
Diam 9½in. Mark: No 13 in red. Date: c 1805-15.

62 *(above right) Porcelain dessert dish.*
Square-shaped dessert dish with indented corners, magnificently gilded on the rim with an elaborate pattern, and decorated in enamel colours in the centre with a finely detailed painting of fruits and foliage on a table. This painting has been attributed by the Museum to Thomas Steel (see p 94).
Width 8½in. Mark: No 15a in red. Date: c 1810-20.
Victoria and Albert Museum

63 *(below) Porcelain dessert basket stand.*
Stand for matching dessert basket, decorated in overglaze enamels, with gilding on the border. The central enamelled painting is of a Chinese man, woman and child around a table in a garden. They sit under a flowering tree. The man is playing a pipe. The piece has oval-shaped piercing at the rim.
Length 11in. Mark: No 13 in red. Date: c 1805-15.
Hanley Museum, Stoke-on-Trent

The earliest recorded dessert ware pattern number 170 occurs upon a dessert plate magnificently decorated in the Swansea fashion with pink roses and superb gilding. This piece would seem to date from c 1810-15. No pattern number is recorded for the service pictured in (64), which is much more clearly attributable to the 1812-20 period when the painting of botanical specimens on both earthenware and porcelain was particularly fashionable, and had been brought to a high degree of perfection at Swansea, Nantgarw and Derby. Also dating from the 1815-20 period is the finely enamelled dessert dish (62). Again it is in a style recognisably Swansea or Derby in origin.

The rarity of marked 'Longport' pieces, which seem to date from before c 1812, leads to the conclusion that much of the early porcelain dessert ware was unmarked.

The quality of porcelain potting, certainly up to c 1825, was almost invariably good. One occasionally reads emphatic statements that Davenports made two bodies in this period, a best body which is white and clean in the Sèvres manner, and an inferior body somewhat greyish in paste. This is manifest nonsense. There are more variations in paste or body than can be accurately determined. Within the basic bone china formula many different bodies were produced. However much one would like to be able to say of an unmarked plate, 'That is a Davenport porcelain body,' this is just not possible. What can be said is that some dessert wares were manufactured in a very fine, white and clean body, and that others were rather heavy and grey in appearance. In between these extremes, a wide range of variation occurs in the period up to c 1825.

Not merely pastes and formulas changed in the early nineteenth century, styles of decoration and shapes of wares underwent several cycles of fashion. Neo-classicism as a style was never very suited to porcelain wares, though its influence was manifest. By the early nineteenth century the Empire-line and the Regency influence had brought forth different shapes and different decorations frequently based on those in favour with the silversmith. In time, they too passed, and the simple landscape set in a plain white porcelain background, or the specimen flower framed by a simple coloured border (69), also fell out of fashion. The prevalent style from the mid-

64 *Porcelain dessert service pieces.*
Representative selection from a forty-four piece porcelain botanical dessert service. Each piece is decorated with a finely painted and accurately coloured representation of a different, and named, flowering plant. The green border has a matt finish. The pieces illustrated are: (left) an oval-shaped dish, (centre) a fruit bowl and stand with elaborately pierced rims, and (right) a rectangular side dish. No sizes are known. Mark: 'printed marks in sepia' (presumably 15a or b).
The service comprised a fruit bowl and stand, two sauce tureens covers and stands, four rectangular dishes, four shell dishes and twenty-four plates. It was sold at Sotheby's on 4 February 1969 for £850.
Sotheby & Co

twenties to the mid-thirties, or a little thereafter, was 'revived rococo'. This was a return to a fashion of a previous age, in particular to the style and grace of mid-eighteenth century France. It is a style peculiarly suited to porcelain, but in its 'revived' form in nineteenth-century England it found expression in some garish and over-decorated pots emanating from such highly-esteemed sources as Coalport, Rockingham, Derby, Minton and Spode. Not all their wares merit this description, but a significant proportion does.

The progress of this style may be followed in the four dessert dishes on p 77. The first piece (65) dates from the 1820s and its irregular outline is indicative of neo-rococo influence. The full flower of the style can be seen in (66). There is no repose in this piece, no smooth, sweeping lines and clean-cut finishes—all is restlessness, fussiness and ostentation. It must be stressed, however, that this type of decoration and shape was no worse than some of the absurdities created in the name of art in the eighteenth century. Moreover, the very brashness of the ornamentation employed by the potters of the 1830s is an assertion of their technical mastery over their materials. The rising middle class made rich by the profits of industry were anxious to adorn their newly-built homes with services, vases and other ornamental china, which by the lavishness of its gilding and the richness of its ground colours would astonish their visitors. We may not particularly admire some of the more extravagant fantasies of the period, but we ought to make the effort to understand the cultural climate in which they were produced.

The dish (67) is from the late 1830s and is for a cheaper market than (66) was intended for, but it, too, though simpler in outline, has a great deal more decorative *detail* than would have been likely twenty years previously. Finally, the low dish (68) of similar form to that shown with the part service (71): here is a piece with no recognisable shape. It isn't round or oval or square (it is vaguely five-sided), but it is finely painted, the china is of the highest quality and the gilding good and clean.

It is worth noting the changing convention of flower painting in the two plates (69 and 70). The former is the simple botanical specimen of the 1810-20 period, the latter a more complex arrange-

65 *(above left) Porcelain dessert side dish.*
Footed dish decorated with a semi-matt green border embellished with raised matt and burnished gilding. In the centre an enamel painting in colours of a pink rose bud and a red dahlia. The pierced handles are partially gilt and a gilt border frames the centre.
Length $10\frac{3}{4}$in. Width $8\frac{1}{2}$in. Mark: No 15b. No pattern number, but plates from this service bear the pattern number 292. Date: c 1820-30.
Brian Smith Esq.

66 *(above right) Porcelain dessert side dish.*
Footed dish with elaborately moulded and pierced border in the revived rococo manner in the form of flower heads and scrolls. The sides decorated with four cartouche containing enamel paintings of wild flowers. In the centre framed by a broad gilt band, a bunch of flowers is enamelled, a pink rose and an aster being prominent in this group which is tied with a bright blue ribbon.
Length $10\frac{1}{2}$in. Width 9in. Mark: No 19 printed in puce and pattern number 356. Date: c 1830-35.

67 *(below left) Porcelain dessert side dish.*
Hexagonally-shaped footed dish with moulded edge. On the side, a ground colour of underglaze grey is decorated overglaze with gilt patterns of frond and leaf designs. In the centre a gilt star-shaped motif.
Length 11in. Width 8in. Mark: No 18 in a pinky-grey or puce shade (the printing is very faint) and pattern number 479. Date: c 1835-45.

68 *(below right) Porcelain dessert side dish or low comport.*
Irregularly-shaped side dish with pierced edge and scroll handle. The foot is shaped in one piece and is also pierced. The sides are decorated with detailed net, ribbon and flower chain patterns in gilt over a turquoise green ground. Enamelled in the centre with a finely executed painting of a carnation.
Width $9\frac{1}{2}$in. Height to rim $2\frac{1}{4}$in. Mark: No 16 printed underglaze in blue, pattern number 1119. Date: c 1845-55.

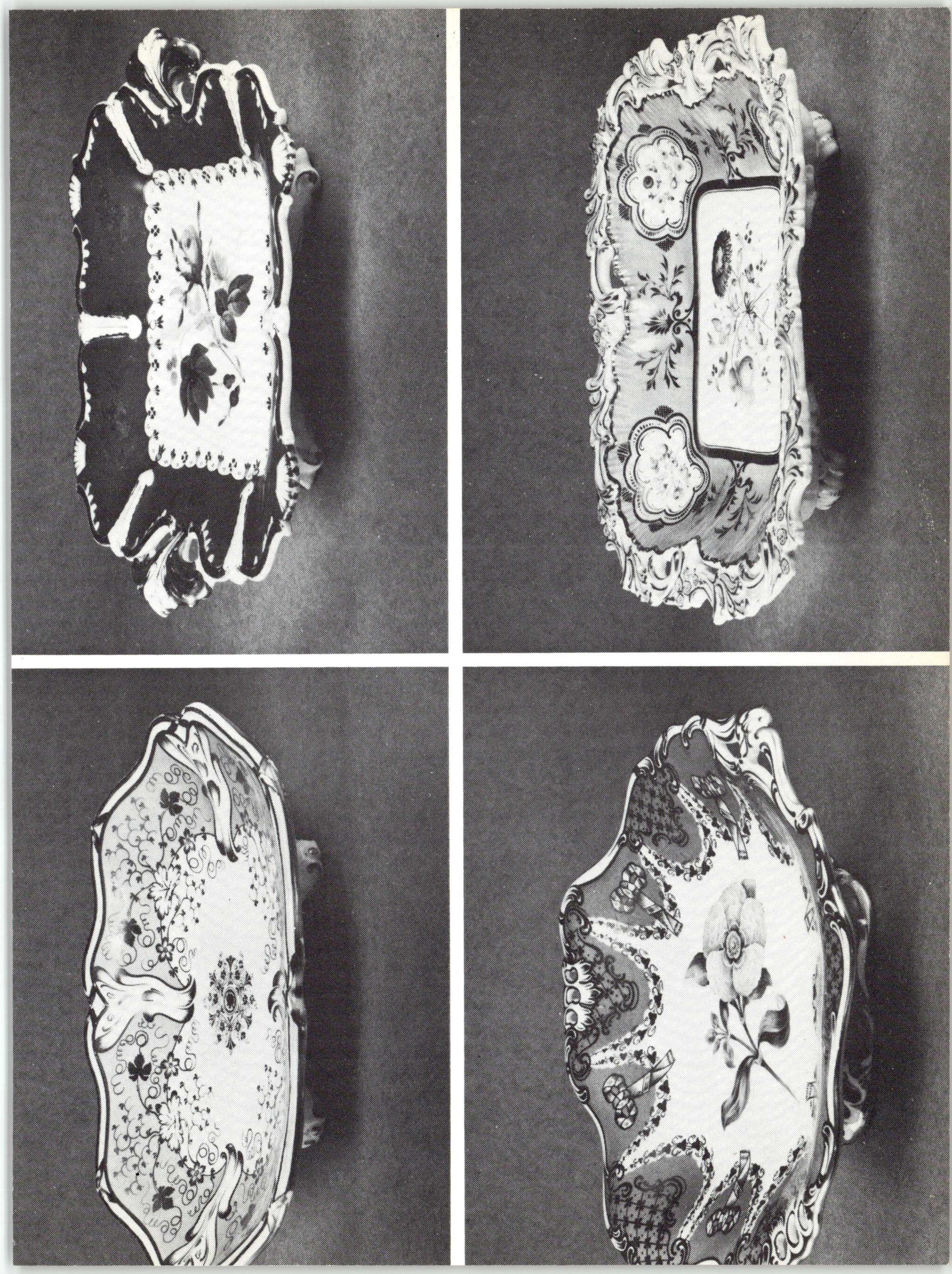

ment of flower groups of the 1820s set in a moulded border common to so many factories, especially Swansea, Nantgarw and Coalport (see G. A. Godden, *Coalport*, colour plate III).

Undoubtedly the *tour de force* of the Davenport factory was the dessert service made to the order of William IV and used at his Coronation Banquet. Both Ward and Jewitt allude to the service, and Ward records that:

> This splendid production was . . . exhibited publicly at the works at Longport, previously to its being forwarded to St James's . . . his Majesty testified, in the warmest manner, his gratification in finding his own country capable of producing such a display of art.

Full details of this fine service which unfortunately is in a rather damaged condition and therefore not normally in current use, are given in the captions on pp 80 and 82. The two illustrations give some indication of the nature of the service, which combines interesting elements of Sèvres taste in the treatment of the border and the reserved panels with more obvious neo-rococo themes in the shapes of the comports and dishes. (It is hoped to publish photographs of all the shapes in the *Transactions of the English Ceramic Circle*, 1973.)

It is particularly gratifying to find in the *Foxley* papers four relevant letters:

> 22nd Nov 1830.
>
> Dear Will,
>
> The King has requested to have the Group completed with a red, & *white* rose, shamrock, thistle, & leek,—tied with the Union Riband—I am getting a drawing made here to save time. I regret my instructions were so badly attended to, for these people don't like trouble—I learn that four or five services are now ordered—we shall I fear be the last to complete his Orders. How is it that so much time has been lost already? You need not do any thing more as the *Bouquet* will be fixed upon—I thought the model sent pretty good, as good as we shall get it—cost 3 Guineas —We can't get anything from Pitts. As to the pyramids ordered by V.D.P. [Victor Pontigny] 20 inches high they must be made in separate trays to be placed on a pillar or Rod which will make them this shape [diagram] this may perhaps allow you to make the shells more ornamental—the largest tray to be 9 inches. Sir Herbert Taylor observed that the *Bouquet*

69 *(above left) Porcelain plate.*
Indented dessert plate decorated with a matt green border edged in gilt. In the centre, a painting in green and yellow enamels of a specimen flower.
Diam $9\frac{1}{2}$*in. Mark: No 14 printed in pale red, and the name of the flower 'Bladder Podded Alyssum'. No pattern number. Date: c 1815-25.*

70 *(above right) Porcelain plate.*
Dessert plate with moulded rim of 'C' scrolls and floral garlands tied with a bow. The border is matt green with gilt outlines, the floral garlands being left white. Also on the rim are six reserved pictures of delicately painted and highly coloured birds. In the centre framed by a deep gilt border, three small, tight sprays of garden flowers are enamelled.
Diam $9\frac{3}{4}$*in. Mark: 15a in green. No pattern number. Date: c 1815-25.*

71 *(below) Pieces from a porcelain dessert service.*
Main pieces from a service decorated throughout with a pale green ground colour enriched with raised gilding. In the centre of each piece a view is enamelled.
Left: Comport centre-dish of irregular shape and pierced rim.
Height $8\frac{1}{2}$*in. Mark: No 18 in puce, pattern number 841.*
Centre: Low comport. See also (68).
Max width $9\frac{1}{4}$*in. Mark and pattern number as above.*
Right: Sauce tureen and cover with elaborate finial.
Height $8\frac{1}{4}$*in. Mark and pattern number as above.*
Date: c 1845-55.

G. A. Godden Esq FRSA

was not done so well as the *Groups* on the Border, nor by the same hand. We shall have trouble with this thing—I believe however that our specimen stands first—Flight & Barr are doing theirs in Blue ground . . .

I am your affect' father

Jn Davenport. (*Foxley*, 79).

Three points deserve mention. Davenport writes of four or five services having been ordered. The two best known are the Rockingham (see A. A. Eaglestone and T. A. Lockett, pp 107-110 for full details, and D. G. Rice for photographs of specimens) and the Flight & Barr service of which a plate may be seen in the Dyson Perrins Museum, Worcester. The fear that the service would be the last completed was unfounded. The Rockingham set took five years to complete, was exhibited in London in 1837 and first used at the Coronation of William's successor, Queen Victoria (T. A. Lockett, 'The Bramelds in London', *The Connoisseur*, June 1967, p 102). The phrase 'we can't get anything from Pitts' may require explanation. William Pitts (b 1790, d 1840) was a sculptor and painter who according to Rupert Gunnis (p 307) assisted in the designing of the royal dessert service. 'In drawing and modelling he was,' says Gunnis, 'ambidextrous and sometimes even used both hands at the same time.'

A week later Davenport wrote again to William:

They will send you tonight a copy for an *Estimate* which is required for the Board of Green Cloth, you must price it and charge well—Lady Stafford said more about cheapness than she ought to have done, some of the other services will cost four times as much—The king said he was *greatly* satisfied with what patterns we had sent him—and wished the flowers as he had got *Arms* and *Crowns* enough on his other Setts (sic)—and that he wanted something more like the old Seve as ours was—I feel sure it will be the most esteemed. (*Foxley*, 80).

Unfortunately no record of the price seems to have survived.

Early in 1831 a further note of urgency crept into the correspondence:

Dear Henry,

You will & must have more time for the execution of the King's service—I have declined for the present sending in any estimate . . . (*Foxley*, 57)

72 *Porcelain comport from the Royal Dessert Service. Comport with centre pillar on a base resting on a separate stand. The dish is decorated with a border composed of a trellis design of ribbon in raised gold on a green ground. Inset are three cartels with enamelled bouquets of flowers. In the centre, framed by gilding, is a bouquet of the national emblems—rose, thistle, shamrock and leek—joined with the Union Ribbon. See (73). Beneath the dish further flowers are enamelled. The moulded centre pillar is decorated with a raised trellis pattern of white porcelain with four-leaf motifs at the crossings; it terminates in heavily gilt moulded leaves which support the dish.*

The base is rectangular with canted corners and is similarly decorated with a green ground, a gilt trellis design and flower groups in reserved panels. On the sides of the base are raised conventional motifs, gilded in parts.

The stand is also rectangular with canted corners. It is decorated with a green ground and lattice scrolls, and a centrally-placed, moulded and gilt shell. It is supported on four inturned scrolls below single shells, all of which are gilded.

Height 14in. Width 12½in. Depth 10in. (There are four similar pieces). Mark: No 15b printed. Date: 1830.

By gracious permission of Her Majesty the Queen

A little later an undated letter to Henry Davenport exemplifies the meticulous attention to the details of pot-making which so distinguished John Davenport from his sons:

I have returned the plate last sent which I think you will allow is still worse managed than the other. The Bouquet is not in the Centre of the plate and the painting which appears over-fired, and some of the remarks with the former plate apply to this—It appears as though some leaves had been rubbed out but not done effectually as the Glaze is stained, the Stems are poor and thin the White Rose not well managed—As to varying the Groups I think as you are confined to subjects, you can hardly do it with effect especially as the ribbon Eye must be always in the same place—the *Eye* of this is not quite in the right place—On the border you will see three rose *tree* leaves all done yellow and exactly the same colour—while one should have been in distance and all a little varied—the same observation applies to the Auriculas and some of the flowers in the Groups—this would cost nothing to remedy—and may be a reason for not varying the Groups. But Will had a full explanation on these points and can attend to them, no more time should be lost. We have not sent any estimate in at present . . .

The letter is endorsed: The centre Groups or Bouquet should be *well done* and all by Gould [or possibly Goold] if possible. (*Foxley*, 58).

The mention of the artist Gould is of interest for it provides an almost unique occasion when the Davenport artists can be identified with certainty. Here we have documentary evidence that William Pitts was to design the shapes of the service and that the centre groups were painted by Gould. Unfortunately, nothing further is known of this artist.

According to a china inventory of 15 February 1855 at Buckingham Palace, the service consisted of 187 pieces, and even then a number of the pieces were damaged and cracked.

Artistically, the Davenport service is simpler in form and outline than the Rockingham. Certainly the Rockingham comports modelled as pineapple, or encrusted with blackberries, or coral and shells, or wheat ears are more spectacular. But if one is to eat off heavily-painted china, then a bouquet of English floral emblems is perhaps preferable to a

73 *Porcelain comport from the Royal Dessert Service. Double-handled oblong low comport or side dish, elaborately neo-rococo in outline with 'C' and 'S' scroll edges and moulded shells at the rim. The handles are moulded in the form of vine leaves and are heavily gilt.*

The dish is decorated as (72) except that it has four reserved cartels not three. It rests on four gilt lion's paw feet.

Height 4½in. Width 13½in. Depth 9¼in. Mark: No 15b. Date: 1830.

The service at present consists of the following pieces all similarly decorated:

102 plates, diam 10in.

8 single-handed shell comports. Vine leaf handle, resting on lion's paw feet. Height 4⅞in, width 11⅞in, depth 11¼in.

7 double-handled oblong comports, as seen here.

6 double-handled round comports. Vine leaf handles, resting on four lion's paw feet. Height 4⅝in, width 13⅛in, depth 11in.

3 comports with covers, on centre pillar, supported by three dolphins. Triangular base, the cover handle is also in the form of three dolphins. Height 12in, diam 8¼in.

4 comports with centre pillar on a base resting on a separate stand. The rectangular base and stand have canted corners, the latter is supported on four inturned scrolls below single shells. Height 14in, width 12¼in, depth 10in.

3 round comports with centre pillar on a round base. Height 11in, diam 11¾in.

One three-tier centre-piece. The tiers are on a centre pillar and are flanked at their base by marine horses and rest on a rectangular stand supported on inturned scrolls. Height 26in.

By gracious permission of Her Majesty the Queen

royal coat of arms, including, as it does, St George slaying the dragon!

In common with other manufacturers Davenports produced wares to the individual order of the nobility and gentry (and according to Scarrett, p 64, for the corporation of the City of Liverpool). Two such service pieces are shown in (74 and 75). Separated by over half a century in date of manufacture, both the Claxson armorial plate of c 1820 and the monogrammed plate of c 1880 display a high standard of potting and finish. In the same way the plates (76 and 77) may be commended. They too are well turned-out. If one sets them beside the *Longport* plate (61), one may see a progression from 1810 through 1850 to 1870 of high-quality finish; of a diminution of the importance of the picture, and the use of much thinner, flatter enamels in the later period.

Marks on dessert wares seem to be frequent after c 1815.

A separate pattern book existed for dessert wares (and another for teawares). The range of dessert patterns may be represented as follows:

Pattern number	*Approximate* date of introduction
150-200	c 1815-20
200-300	c 1820-25
300-400	c 1825-35
400-700	c 1835-45
700-1200	c 1845-55
1200-1700	c 1855-75

Beyond this figure too few patterns have been noted to make even an approximation worthwhile.

74 *(above left) Porcelain armorial plate.*
Armorial plate with broad gold band on the rim and a bright semi-matt mid-blue border, decorated with sprays, roses and insignia in heavy raised and chased gold. In the centre the armorial of the Claxson family is painted in enamel colours. The crest shows a stag with a pennant upon which there is a hedgehog. The motto SAPERE AUDE INCIPE may be translated, 'Dare to be wise, begin.'
Diam 10in. Mark: 15b printed in puce and pattern number 265. Date: c 1820.

75 *(above right) Porcelain monogrammed plate.*
Decorated on the rim with a meandering floral pattern in blue, green and red enamels and gilt. In the centre a monogram SMS in blue, red and gilt.
Diam 10in. Mark: No 22. No pattern number. Date: 1875-85.

76 *(below left) Porcelain plate.*
Wavy-edged plate, pierced on the rim in three places with groups of three holes. The rim decorated with a gilt scroll motif, and in the centre a country scene is enamelled in colour.
Diam $9\frac{1}{2}$in. Mark: No 16 printed in blue underglaze. Pattern number 918. Date: c 1845-55.

77 *(below right) Porcelain plate.*
Decorated with a maroon border ornamented with a gilt pattern. In the centre there is an enamel painting in colours of a ruin beside a lake or river.
Diam $9\frac{1}{2}$in. Mark: No 18 printed in red and pattern number 1649. Date c 1870-80.

SAPERE AUDE INCIPE

TEAWARES

From the beginning of porcelain manufacture, there must have been a considerable output of teawares from the Longport factory. Unfortunately, as was noted with the dessert wares, these early products have not been identified. The only marked piece of what might be termed teaware known to the author, is the very fine covered cabinet cup and saucer (78). This piece from the Victoria & Albert Museum is excellently decorated in the style of c 1805-10. It is the equal of anything produced contemporaneously at Derby, Minton or Spode. However, it stands alone at this stage of research.

The types of ware which might repay close scrutiny are the 'cottagey' pseudo-New Hall tea bowls and saucers in soft paste or bone china, and the coffee cans, jugs and tea pots in the style of early Spode or Minton teawares. This is indeed a difficult area, for the first decade or so of the nineteenth century saw the production of many high-class but unmarked (or rarely marked) porcelain wares. For example, much of the work of Miles Mason was unrecognised until the recent researches of Reginald Haggar. One can only hope that a few marked examples will be discovered of early Davenport which will enable accurate attribution of unmarked pieces to be made on the basis of shape and pattern.

Turning to the wares of which we have knowledge, the lowest recorded pattern number occurs on the jug and sucrier (79). It should be stressed at the outset that a separate pattern book existed for tea and dessert wares, though very occasionally an identical pattern might appear on both types of ware. The jug and sucrier have a very distinctive shape, they are marked with pattern number 327 and date from the period 1810-15. How much below this number the patterns ran is not easy to say. No pattern books are known to exist, and though it is logical to assume that a factory would begin at pattern number 1, it is more likely in practice that patterns would be designed and used before any official pattern book was compiled. When this happened it may have been difficult to fill in all the gaps, or more politic from the sales point of view to start the pattern book at, say, pattern 200 or some such figure. This would give the customer confidence that the factory had a well-established stock of patterns. Not all firms

78 *(above) Porcelain covered cup and saucer/stand. Decorated with gilt patterns over all three pieces. On the cover two scenes are enamelled of ruins which are set in irregularly-shaped gilt frames. On the cup the scroll handles are gilded and on each side of the body an eight-sided panel in gilt, frames an enamel-coloured view. On the reverse side it is of a ruined Gothic building; on the front there is a distant view of St Paul's.*
Total width 6in. Height $4\frac{3}{4}$in. Diam of saucer 6in. Mark: No 13 painted in red. No pattern number. Date: c 1805-10.
Victoria and Albert Museum

79 *(below) Porcelain sugar box and cream jug.*
Left: Sugar box decorated with a bold leaf pattern in gold. The handles have three distinct prongs or points where they start from on the body and at their highest point they divide into two and continue a little way on either side along the shoulders of the vessel. The top of the finial is moulded as a four-petalled flower.
Overall length 8in. Height 5in. Mark: No 15a printed very faintly in red and pattern number 327 in gold. Date: c 1810-15.
Right: Cream jug similarly decorated with a split handle in the same form as the sucrier.
Overall length 6in. Height $3\frac{3}{4}$in. No mark, pattern number 327 in gold (very faint). Date: c 1810-15.
Brian Smith Esq

acted thus, but some undoubtedly did. Furthermore, it is often forgotten that potters did *not* make their pots for subsequent collectors. The order and regularity which the connoisseur and collector bring to their catalogues and learned monographs was not the spirit in which most of the pots were made. In overcrowded and filthy workshops, tired, semi-literate and sometimes half-drunk workmen did not bring to their work the passionate devotion to regularity and consistency which is the desideratum of certain modern scholars. Marks in the 'wrong' colour, pattern numbers which do not tally, scenes painted by 'another hand' or in unusual colours, these and many other faults are far more frequent than we like to allow. The potter would be astonished to see that some of his 'mistakes' are the subject of learned articles, and that perversely they enhance rather than detract from the value (whatever that might mean!) of his pots.

The change to a greater frequency of marks appears to have come in the 1815-20 period. Wares from this period are much more plentiful and several different shapes can be assigned to the decade 1815-25. Prominent are those shown in (80). The cup shape is very similar to Spode's *London* shape which was introduced c 1813. As this shape was also used by Minton, New Hall, Coalport, Charles Bourne, the Grainger and Chamberlain factories at Worcester and possibly several other makers, the attribution of unmarked wares is fraught with difficulty. Small differences in the moulding of the wares of the various firms do exist, but it is not easy to identify, say, an unmarked cream jug at sight. The *exact* moulded shape must be memorised and the significant details such as the very small spur (by comparison with other makers) on the inside of the handle on the Davenport teapot, sucrier and cream jug need to be borne in mind. The pattern number should also provide assistance. That of the pieces illustrated (80) is 554 and this almost automatically rules out a Spode attribution, for by the date when this service was made Spode patterns had reached at least 2,500. This would not necessarily apply to Minton, the shape of whose cups is remarkably like those of Davenport (see G. A. Godden, *Minton*, col plates II and plate 15). Minton patterns were still under 1,000 by 1815. Coalport, too, were in this range, pattern 629 is

80 *Porcelain tea service.*

Representative pieces from a porcelain tea service decorated in deep blue underglaze, with an overglaze pattern in gilt of a ribbon, garland and flower sprays.

Dimensions:

Tea cup. Height 2¼in. Diam 3½in.
Saucer. Diam 5½in.
Teapot. Length 10½in.
Slop bowl. Height 3¼in.
Sucrier. Height 4½in. Overall length 7½in.

Mark: No 16 printed overglaze in red. Pattern number 554. Date: c 1815-25.

G. A. Godden Esq FRSA

illustrated in Godden's *Encyclopaedia*, plate 164.

Three other comparatively early teaware shapes are illustrated in the group of wares (83). The left cup has a squarish form of handle quite common in the 1820s. In a Rockingham version the top of the handle does not project above the rim of the cup, but other factories produced fluted cups of similar form. The cup and saucer on the right of (83) are of pattern 730, one of the specialities of the factory. Here again unmarked specimens are fairly frequently encountered in this *Etruscan* shape (a Davenport piece with a different handle is illustrated in G. V. Bemrose, plate 58A). Pattern numbers are again helpful, for the similar Spode specimen is pattern 3614 whilst the Coalport example (see Godden, *Coalport* plate 152 and *Encyclopaedia* plate 167) is of a somewhat different shape in profile. Perhaps enough has been said of the pitfalls of 'instant attribution' to warn collectors that there is no substitute for a detailed and accurate knowledge of the shapes and pattern numbers of the various factories.

The regimental saucer (83) is another reminder of the vast overseas market served by Davenport (examples of a more elaborate Mess service for the '49th Regiment' are known). The floral-decorated saucer on the left is an example of the delicacy of potting and skill in painting that from time to time was achieved at the factory. This piece is every bit as good as a comparable Swansea specimen.

The pieces of the service (81) take us into the 1830s and the revived rococo fashion. The particularly distinctive features about this fairly common set of shapes are the handles to the cups which have not been encountered from any other factory. Teapots with similar animal spouts and broad shoulders were made by Coalport, but the form of the Davenport handle is again slightly different (see Godden, *Coalport*, plates 162 and 165).

A rather rarer type of ware dating from the 1830-37 period is (82). The finish is particularly fine with gilding of the highest class. Several similar mugs and saucers decorated with ground colours and heavy lattice-work gilding are in the Hanley Museum collection. Curiously enough, although these pieces are marked none bears a pattern number.

Two further illustrations in this section (84 and 85) show a range of teawares from the late 1830s

81 *Porcelain tea service.*

Representative pieces of a porcelain tea service decorated with a pale green underglaze ground colour, and with elaborate overglaze gilt patterns. There are small roses enamelled at intervals round the pieces. The rims are lightly moulded in a scroll and shell pattern.

Dimensions:

Plate. Diam 8¼in.
Saucer. Diam 6in.
Cups, (left: coffee). Height to rim 2¼in,
(right: tea).
Height to rim 2in.
Slop bowl. Height 3¼in.
Cream jug. Height 5½in.
Teapot. Height 7¾in.
Sucrier. Height 6½in.

Mark: No 19 printed overglaze in puce. Pattern number 869. Date: 1830-37.

G. A. Godden Esq FRSA

to about 1860. Full descriptions of decoration are given in the captions, but particular attention is directed to the handle shapes, of which the flattened ring handle on two of the cups in (85) is the most frequently encountered. The shape was registered in 1849 and continued in use for over a decade. The wares from the 1870s and 80s will be mentioned in the concluding section (see p 100).

So far very little has been said of the artists who decorated Davenport porcelain. The main reason for this is a paucity of information. As no factory ledgers, wage books or pattern books are known to have survived, no unpublished list of painters, gilders, modellers and decorators is available. This is unfortunate as it would be pleasant to pay suitable tribute to the Davenport artists whose skill still delights us. The only names that have been linked with the factory are those listed in the Mankowitz and Haggar *Encyclopaedia*, p 67 and in Geoffrey Godden's *Victorian Porcelain*, p 198. To these a further few names and details can be added:

ABLOTT, Richard (c 1870-80), landscape artist, formerly at Derby.

AUSTIN, Jesse (b 1806), engraver and designer, said to have been apprenticed at Davenports (see p 56).

BROOKES, William (d 1838), engraver. See p 50 and W. L. Little, pp 53-4, for details.

CAPEY, R. (c 1875-85), landscape painter (see p 104).

CLOWES, William (c 1803), according to Jewitt (Vol II, p 284) was a worker at Davenports. Later he became co-founder with Hugh Bourne of the Primitive Methodists (see p 106).

CRISTALL, Joshua, water-colour painter, said to have served his time at the factory.

CUTTS, James (c 1840-60), engraver of blue printed patterns (see p 54, and Scarrett p 170 for a picture of Cutts and his house).

EATON, R. (c 1880), floral artist.

FLETCHER, W., figure painter. Two signed plates of his in the V. and A. were formerly attributed to Davenport (illustrated in Mankowitz and Haggar, plate 37, bottom row). Godden, *Coalport*, p 137-8, attributes these plates to Coalport. This seems correct, Fletcher ought not to be regarded as a Davenport artist.

GOULD (c 1830), floral artist and decorator of the royal dessert service (see p 82).

82 *(above) Porcelain coffee can and saucer. Decorated with a deep royal blue ground painted underglaze, inset with reserves in red. Within the panels a classical figure subject has been left in white. The oval panels are surrounded by raised gilding in scrollwork and leaf forms. Simple loop handle on mug. Cup height 2⅜in. Saucer diam 5⅛in. Mark: No 19 in puce. No pattern number. Date: c 1830-35.*

Hanley Museum, Stoke-on-Trent

83 *(below) Porcelain teawares c 1820-30.*

Top (left to right). (i) Fluted coffee cup decorated with simple printed outline flower pattern, filled-in with green enamel. Height 2½in. Mark: No 16 in red. Pattern 394. Date: c 1820.

Mrs. Elsie Blatch.

(ii) Tea cup decorated with simple five-petal pink flowers and well-executed gilt foliage. Height 2in. Mark: No 16 in red. Pattern 709. Date: c 1820-25.

(iii) Coffee cup decorated with two bands of navy blue underglaze, and overglaze with pale yellow floral reserves outlined in gilt. Height 2¾in. Mark: No 16 in brown. No pattern number. Date: c 1825.

(iv) Cup with saucer (below it) finely enamelled in pink with six full-blown roses and several rose buds, with rich additional gilded patterns. Cup height 1¾in. Saucer diam 6¼in. Mark No 16 in red. Pattern 730. Date: c 1820-25.

(v) (bottom left) Saucer moulded on the rim with 'C' scrolls, flower and ribbon patterns (see 70 also) and finely painted with a floral bouquet and four single flowers near the rim. Diam 5⅞in. Mark: No 16 in red. Pattern 706. Date: c 1820-25.

(vi) Saucer decorated with a gilt-lined rim, royal blue underglaze ground and a gilt motif framing the well which is enamelled with a coat-of-arms. This shows a crown surmounting a garter wreath with the words '1st Madras Fusiliers', a leopard is painted in the centre; beneath is a garland ribbon with the words SPECTAMUR AGENDO. Diam 5½in. Mark: No 16 in brown. Pattern 508. Date: uncertain, but probably c 1825.

HOLLAND, James (b 1799, d 1870), water-colour painter, said to have been apprenticed at Davenports. Some of his art work is in the Hanley Museum collection.

LESSORE, Emile, known to have decorated Davenport porcelain (see p 108).

LUCAS, Daniel (sen.) (b 1777), 'in early life a painter at Davenports' (Scarrett, p 166).

MARSH, James, modeller, mid-century.

MOUNTFORD, Jesse (c 1834-61), landscape painter from Derby and Coalport (see Godden, *Coalport*, p 137 and *Victorian*, plate 99).

PITTS, William (b 1790, d 1840), worked on designs for royal service.

SLATER, William (sen.) (1784-1864), according to Scarrett (p 112) was an apprentice at Pinxton, moved to Derby and after a varied career came to Davenports in c 1848 as a gilder and ornamental painter.

SLATER, William (jun.) (1807-65), according to Scarrett the eldest son of the above, designer and manager at the firm for 'upwards of 32 years'.

STEELE, Edwin (1805-71), known to have worked at Derby and Rockingham (there c 1828-32), then moved to Staffordshire. Traditionally alleged to have worked at Davenports. The vase (90) is in his style (see Godden, *Minton*, p 124).

STEEL(E), Thomas (c 1771-1850), worked at Derby, Rockingham and Mintons. Said to have worked for Davenports, but the plaque illustrated by Bemrose, plate 70 is of Minton manufacture. The dish (62) is usually attributed to him (see Godden, *Minton*, pp 124-6).

Note: the name Steel occurs in the *Foxley* correspondence eg in 1812 'young Steel' is to be kept in order at Liverpool; 'he marches to Burslem if he offends again.' By 1828 Steele is being granted 'a power of attorney' to deal with an account opened at a new bank. In 1831 Steele is reported to be abroad and auction sales of china are contemplated in his absence. It seems clear from the context that the Steel(e) in question was connected with the business and not the artistic side of the concern.

The last pieces in this section are the teapot and jugs on p 97. The teapot (86) is really an extraordinary piece. If it did not bear the 1830-37 mark, No 19, then one would almost certainly place it as a mid-Victorian extravaganza. It is in fact another expression of the neo-rococo mood. Pieces in a similar vein are the well-known Obadiah Sherratt

84 *(above) Porcelain teawares c 1830-45.*

(i) (Top and bottom left) Cup and saucer, pale green ground and elaborate gilt scroll and tracery design. Cup height 2in, saucer diam 5¾in. Mark: No 18 in pink-puce, pattern 1266. Date: c 1840-45.

(ii) Cup with basket-work-type band of printed blue enamel and gilt. Height 2¼in. Mark: No 21, pattern 1098. Date: c 1840.

(iii) Cup, pale green ground, and rather sketchy flowers following faintly printed outlines. Traces of gilding. Height 2in. Mark: No 18 in pink-puce, pattern 1225. Date: c 1840-45.

(iv) Cup and saucer (below) with flowers in pink lustre and foliage in green and red enamel. Cup height 2in, saucer diam 5½in. Mark: None, pattern 701. See (55) also. Date: c 1845.

(v) Saucer with diamond-shaped cross-hatched pattern in green, and three finely painted flowers near the rim and a small rose bouquet in the centre. Heavily gilded. Diam 6in. Mark: No 19, pattern 1021. Date: 1830-37.

85 *(below) Porcelain teawares c 1850-70.*

(i) Coffee cup, moulded and fluted body, flattened ring handle. Decoration; alternate stripes of mid-blue and green enamel (seven of each) overlaid with gilt tracery. Height 2½in. Mark: No 20 in blue, no pattern number. Date: c 1850-55.

(ii) Coffee cup, moulded and fluted body, ring handle. Decoration: a turquoise stripe and panels of dark cream overlaid with gilt patterns. Height 2¼in. Mark: No 16 underglaze in blue, pattern 2567. Date: c 1855-65.

(iii) Mug with three small stylised flower fronds in underglaze blue. Height 2½in. Mark: 'Davenport' in script in underglaze blue, no pattern number. Date: c 1870.

(iv) Cup and saucer, moulded and fluted body, flattened ring handle. Decoration; a strong tangerine-orange ground with 'C' scrolls and leaf patterns outlined in gilt. Height 2¼in. Mark: No 20, pattern 2144. Date: c 1850-55.

(v) Saucer with gilt dentil edge, three gilded leaf patterns and three scroll patterns in gilt, with an enamel painted harbour scene. Diam 5½in. Mark: No 16 in underglaze blue, pattern 2909. Date: c 1855-65.

(vi) Breakfast saucer with printed scale patterns over an underglaze 'oven' blue ground, also overglaze green, orange and red enamels in a crude chinoiserie design. Diam 6½in. Mark: No 16 printed in black, pattern 2829. Date: c 1860-70.

figure of Neptune standing on a veritable mountain of sea shells and the Rockingham cups and saucers modelled as sea shells (see Mankowitz and Haggar, plate 101, bottom right). Another curious Davenport item, a shell jug in earthenware is illustrated in Hudson Moore, plate 137. According to the text (most of which is highly inaccurate concerning Davenport) the jug is date-marked for 1838, which makes it roughly contemporary with the porcelain teapot. The two jugs (87 and 89) have interesting shapes which collectors would do well to memorise. The small jug (88) is probably of pattern 730 and is delightfully elegant in shape. A teapot for this service was recently noted. It was roughly of barrel-shape, six inches high with a loop handle at the highest point of which was a thumb rest.

The body and glaze of Davenport bone china in the 1830s and 1840s was very good indeed. William Evans (p 62 of the reprint) gives the formula:

DAVENPORTS CHINA BODY

12 lbs bone, 8 lbs 13 oz stone, 5 lbs 9½ oz china clay, 2 lbs 7 oz blue clay, 1 lb 9½ oz flint, ¼ oz blue calx.

DAVENPORTS GLAZE TO CHINA BODY

56 lbs stone, 16 of borax, 15 of flint, 60 of lead, 18 of glass.

This produced a fine white body uniformly glazed.

Finally, the teaware pattern number range may be roughly represented as follows:

Pattern number	*Approximate* date of introduction
300-500	c 1810-20
500-800	c 1820-30
800-1200	c 1830-40
1200-2000	c 1840-50
2000-3000	c 1850-65

Beyond this too few examples have been noted to make even an approximation worthwhile. As a guide, one of the highest recorded numbers—pattern 4,080 was noted on a cup and saucer definitely dating from the 1880s. (Pattern 6,066 recorded on plate 102 is somewhat eccentric and has been disregarded).

The above table is only a rough guide as pieces may be decorated in a pattern long after its first introduction. A significant proportion of marked wares before 1840 have been noted without pattern numbers. Equally some wares carry the factory pattern number, but are otherwise unmarked. Negligence rather than deliberate policy must be the reason for these discrepancies.

86 *(above left) Porcelain shell-shaped teapot.*
Moulded and fluted in the shape of a shell, with the handle and spout coloured and modelled as coral. Further coral strands link the handle and spout. Two freizes of gilding ornament the body which in addition bears four well-executed enamelled flower groups. The lid has a gilt freize, three enamelled flower groups, and the finial in the form of a pink shell, touched with yellow at the base.
Overall height 5½in, total width 7¼in. Mark: No 19 in puce. Date: 1830-37.

87 *(above right) Porcelain jug.*
The bucket-shaped base is moulded in relief with a flower group and decorated overglaze with a floral spray in blue enamel. The neck is flared and rises to a wide mouth. The handle is in the form of a snake. Gilding on the rims and handle.
Total height 9½in. Mark: No 16 overglaze in red, pattern number 1161. Date: c 1835-40.

88 *(below left) Porcelain cream jug.*
Elegantly shaped jug set on a small circular foot. Decorated with a broad band of roses enamelled in pink, with additional buds in pink and foliage in gilt. Gilding on rims, lip, handle and base.
Overall height 6½in. Mark No 16 overglaze in brown, no pattern number. Date: c 1820-25. See (83 iv) also.
Elizabeth Collard, Montreal

89 *(below right) Porcelain jug.*
The circular gilt-lined base supports a fluted and panelled barrel-shaped body. The neck is likewise fluted and the wavy rim follows the line of the fluting. The rococo handle has a scrolled thumb-piece, and facing spurs inside and outside at mid-handle. Decorated with simple, unsophisticated sprays of enamelled daisy-like flowers, and gilding.
Height 7in. Mark: No 16 overglaze in red, pattern number 716. Date: c 1825-35.

ORNAMENTAL WARES—VASES

One of the most puzzling aspects of research into Davenport production is the mystery of the missing vases! The report of the 1806 visit of the Prince of Wales (see p 10) is quite specific: 'of the ornamental parts of the Manufactory HRH was pleased to say that the Vases, Urns &c in point of execution and Ornament were Unique in their kinds.' None of the vases so far located, some of which are illustrated here, dates from the period of the Prince's visit or even to the first decade of the nineteenth century—all are later. One can only presume that the early decorative wares were never marked. Geoffrey Godden quotes the case of Herbert Minton in explanation of why a prominent potter might leave even his finest wares unmarked. Apparently, the china retailers did not like wares to bear the name of the factory of origin, if such marks appeared the customers could go direct to the manufacturers for relacements or new orders (Godden, *Minton*, p 15).

It could also be the case that John Davenport was concerned solely to *sell* his wares and refrained from marking in case the comparative novelty of his firm was held against its products. Or perhaps as Leonard Whiter hints (*Spode*, p 82) he was one of those manufacturers whose wares, resembling those of Sèvres, sold better if prospective customers were not disillusioned and directed to their true origin by a mark.

If Davenport acted from any of these reasons then further detailed research will be necessary to authenticate the missing early wares.

Even after about 1820 marked vases are very rare. The piece shown in (90) is of such superb quality of workmanship that it is hardly credible that a factory capable of producing such a fine thing did not make many similar pieces. But again companion pieces are not in evidence. We are forced to deduce a dearth of marks for the 1820-40 period also. It is possible, however, that certain well-known but unmarked pieces are of Davenport origin. Two vases in the V. and A. (see Mankowitz and Haggar, *Encyclopaedia*, plate 102) were formerly attributed to Rockingham and Edwin Steele. There are good reasons for rejecting them as Rockingham products, and the same applies to another pair of vases in the V. and A. (Mankowitz and Haggar, plate 101, top shelf). Might these anonymous pieces be of Davenport manufacture?

90 *Porcelain vase.*

Vase in the French style. Set on a square plinth the circular base leads to an ovoid body. On the front a tooled gold frame encircles a panel decorated in enamel colours with a basket of luxuriant flowers and fruit resting upon a table.

On the reverse side an elaborate scroll pattern is worked in tooled and burnished gold.

The handles are in the form of grotesque animal heads. The neck is decorated with detailed scroll and cornucopia patterns in gold. The handles, base and rim are all covered in heavy, burnished gold.

It has been suggested that Edwin Steele was responsible for the enamel painting. Though clearly in his style, this would not be an easy attribution to establish securely.

Height 13¾in. Mark: No 16 printed in red. Date: c 1820.

G. A. Godden Esq FRSA

There appears to be no conclusive evidence. All we have is a goodly number of factories to which they definitely do *not* belong. However, one is again forced to say that considerably more research is needed before this period of Davenport's ornamental production can be written about with confidence.

Plate (91) depicts a rose-water ewer, or eau-de-cologne bottle, in the revived rococo style. The encrusted flowers are typical of contemporary wares from Coalport, Rockingham, Minton and Spode. It is interesting to find in the *Foxley* papers (*Foxley* 123) a reference to such wares in a letter from John to Joseph Davenport.

London 23 Oct 1831

> I have been thinking of recommending to you the sending over for your Xmas sales a quantity of these *new things* in raised flowers—as baskets, boxes, cups and stands & etc in imitation of Dresden & which are now selling very cheap—in addition to any of our own make we could buy from Rose & Co & others to form a complete variety—You can give them some ideas at Longport—I feel something would answer, if not they can come back at a trifling expense . . .

At the top of the letter is added:

6 Baskets
12 Eau de Cologne Bottles
12 Toilets
12 Inkstands.

Obviously the ewer was not unique in being fashioned in the popular flower-encrusted manner.

The Empire-style vase (93) positively dates from the 1830-37 period, bearing as it does the 'Royal' mark (No 19, p 111). Although stylistically it may not entirely appeal to modern tastes, the painting and gilding are of the highest quality. The fourth vase depicted (92) is late in date, c 1855, and again in form is imitative of the wares of Sèvres. It is very large and within the conventions of the period most skilfully if laboriously painted.

Other ornamental vases noted include a pair of small vases and covers with a pale blue background and an enamelled panel. These are to be seen in the V. and A., and one is pictured on the bottom row of plate 37 in Mankowitz and Haggar.

A number of vases from the late (1870-80) period decorated with Japan patterns have been noted,

91 *(above) Encrusted porcelain ewer or eau-de-cologne bottle.*
One of a pair of rose-water ewers or eau-de-cologne bottles, set on a square plinth with an acanthus-leaf moulded base rising to an ovoid body which is encrusted with coloured flowers. Enamel flower paintings are found on the foot, body, neck and under the lip. The handle is in the form of a grotesque winged animal. The whole piece is embellished with heavy, burnished gilding.
Height 11½in. Mark: No 16 overglaze in red. Date: c 1830-35.
Victoria and Albert Museum

92 *(below) Porcelain vase.*
Large vase and cover decorated with four reserved panels in enamel colours with lavish floral bouquets. Two further narrow panels decorate the neck of the vase. The lid is likewise enriched with four enamel floral paintings. The panels are surrounded by an elaborate pattern of gilt whorls and dots. Animal motifs in gilt form the handles and finial.
Height 19in. Mark: No 3 impressed. Date: c 1850-60.
The Castle Museum, Nottingham

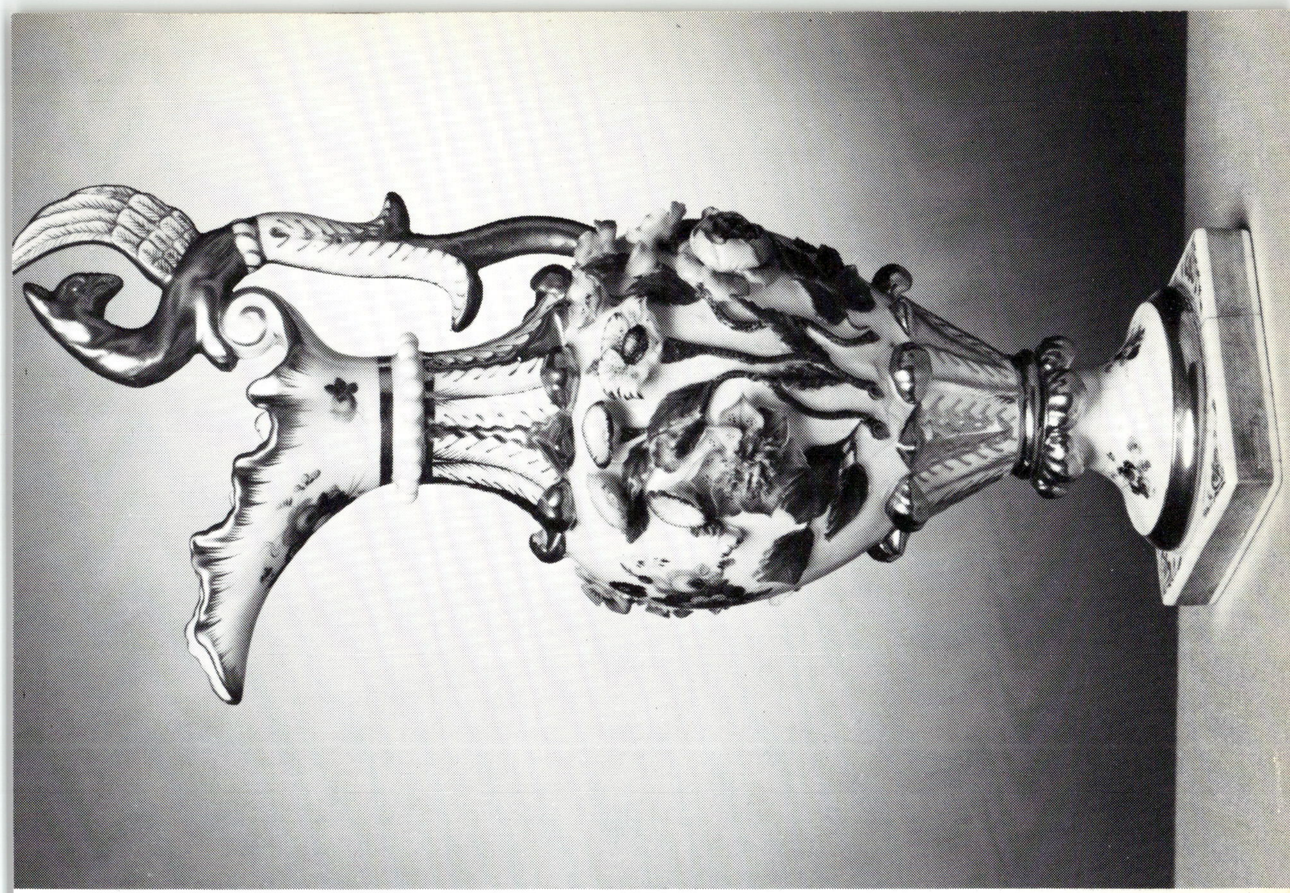

and these and some other later ornamental wares are mentioned on p 108. But even these late wares are by no means plentiful.

It is to be hoped that the publication of this first general book devoted to the factory will serve to encourage keen collectors to undertake research. Perhaps by making detailed comparisons many more pieces will be discovered, so that in a few years' time some of the anonymous vases may be correctly assigned to their factory of origin—Davenport of Longport.

Miscellaneous Decorative Porcelain and the Later Wares

This last general section is devoted to some of the more unusual items of interest to the collector, and to a brief note on the later porcelain wares.

The first two illustrations (94 and 95) are of tea wares that are so decorative that they may stand alone as ornaments quite apart from their original function. The cup and saucer are very rare. The decorative technique of 'stopping-out' a pattern from the ground colour has also been seen on a pair of small blue-ground vases. The same principle has been used on the sucrier (95) to give the decorator a white surface behind some of the enamelled flowers. Ornate cabinet cups of a different form to that in (94) may be seen in the British Museum (see R. L. Hobson, p 147, items XIV 3-7).

The bough or bulb pot (96) is also a rare piece, though it has been suggested that similar pots might exist representing the other continents. The treatment of the subject is somehow rather skittish but particularly attractive. A pair of bough pots in a rather greyish paste, finely decorated with flower groups with the impressed mark No 3 was illustrated in *Collectors Guide*, July 1970, p 23.

The small decorative items in (97) cover almost a fifty-year span. The earliest is the pastille burner. The finish of this piece is excellent, and the eleven separate flower groups are finely executed. A slightly larger size has also been noted decorated with pink roses and gilding. Spode produced similar wares (shape 87, 'Pyramid incense burner' from the 1820 *Shape Book*, reproduced in Whiter, p 99) and a Worcester example may be seen at the Dyson Perrins Museum. The quill and ink set in the form of a miniature teapot is also a charming

93 *(above) Porcelain vase.*
Vase in the Empire style, with square plinth and fluted base. The body of the vase is deeply fluted into panels which are elaborately decorated in enamel colours with flowers and birds. The heavy handles are covered in burnished gold. There are matt gold flower sprays in reserved panels at the top of the flutings.
Height 14½in. Mark: No 19 in puce. Date: c 1830-37.
Mr and Mrs J. K. des Fontaines

94 *(below left) Porcelain specimen cup and saucer.*
Cabinet cup in the French taste heavily gilded at the rims, on the handle and within the cup. Both cup and saucer are decorated with a band of royal blue ground colour on which a stencilled reserve pattern of birds and trees has been lightly enamelled over in places in grey.
Height of cup 2½in, saucer diam 5in. Mark: No 16 overglaze in red. Date: c 1815-20.
Victoria and Albert Museum

95 *(below right) Porcelain sucrier.*
The plain white ground is heavily gilt in delicate leaf patterns and a motif of linked circles. The handles and the finial are gilt. The pale blue ground of the upper body and lid are decorated with enamel paintings of English flower groups, three on the body, two on the lid and a very small group on either side of the finial. Overall length 7½in, height 4½in. Mark: No 14 overglaze in red, no pattern number. Date: c 1810-20.

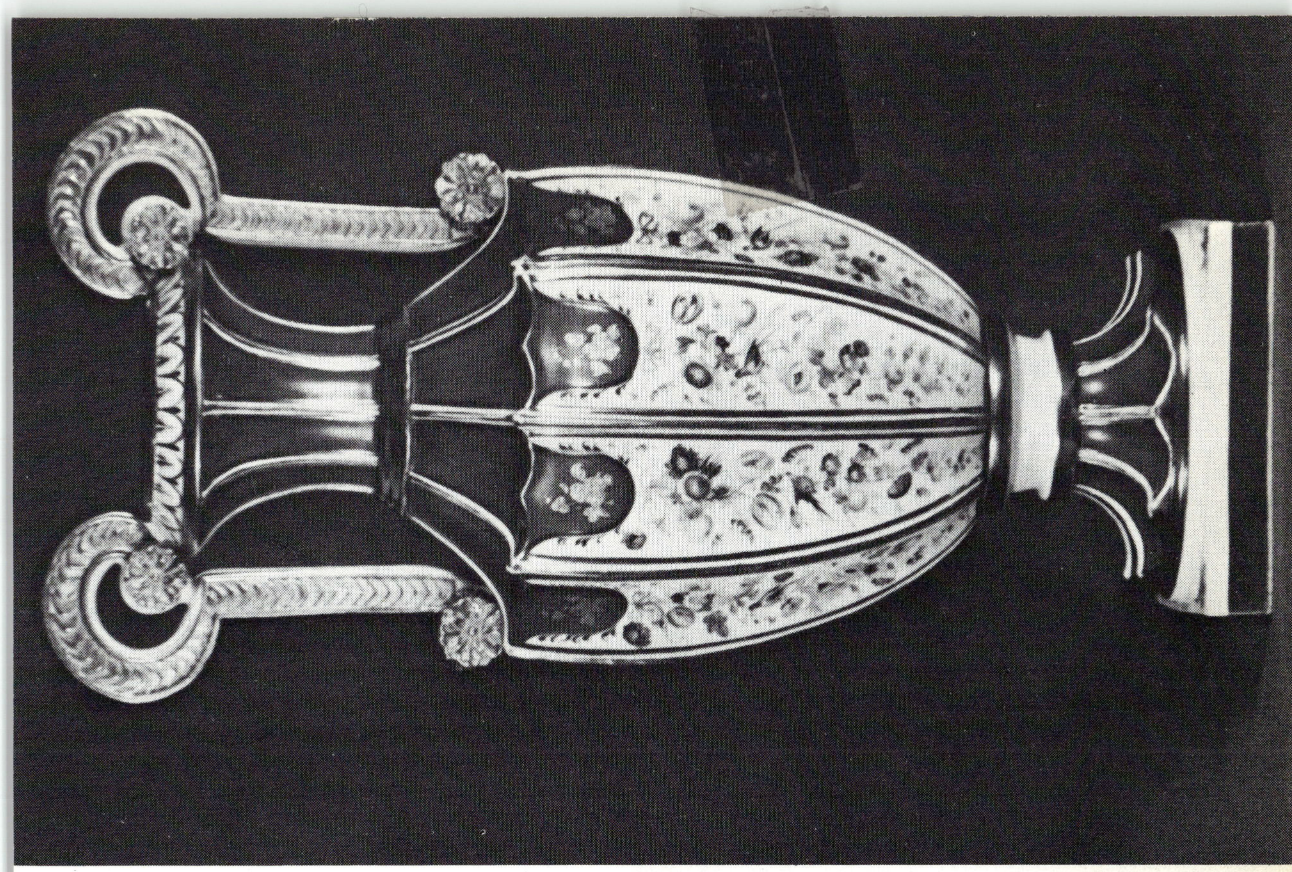

trifle. A slightly larger ink stand of a canoe shape, brilliantly gilded and painted with a pink rose pattern similar to teaware pattern 730 is in a private collection. The frilled-rim vase on tripod feet is very much later in date (c 1870-80). The painting which encircles the piece is of good quality, and serves as a reminder that the lowering of standards noted in connection with the earthenwares did not occur with the majority of later porcelain wares. Even a comparatively trivial piece such as this small vase received careful treatment. Although the mechanical slickness of manufacture may deter those who prefer their pots to possess the hallmarks of craft rather than industry, there can be no denying the technical merit of the later Davenport porcelain. A recently-noted low comport dish enamelled with a flower-spray and supported on a dolphin-tripod stand, comes to mind as an example of the mastery of their skills shown by the later Davenport potters. It may not be art, but it is industrial potting of a very high standard. By the same token the jardinière (99) is a well-turned-out piece (An unusual pair, c 1830 were recently noted, each had four panels decorated with good enamel painted scenes or figure groups in the French style.) Likewise, a magnificent large tray c 1850, green ground and heavily gilt with an enamelled view of Salisbury Cathedral could not be faulted on technical grounds.

Occasionally, framed porcelain slabs may be found painted as though the ware was a canvas. Most factories made these porcelain 'tiles' as they were called, but the Davenport pieces usually bear the mark, DAVENPORT'S PATENT. Rarely was the decoration carried out in the factory, the tiles would be sold to amateurs to try their skill upon, or to professional artists who wished to work in a different medium. Three examples of such plaques were sold at Sotheby's (9 February 1965, lots 59 and 60) these were by S. Chesters, and one piece was signed and dated 23 January 1849. Chesters was a London artist who exhibited enamel portraits and copies of Old Masters at the Royal Academy 1849-1885.

In the 1870s and 80s, circular porcelain plaques were made. Two of those noted have been signed R. Capey. One, a view of Little Moreton Hall entitled *Deserted*, is in the Sadler collection; the second depicted a view of Coniston Lake. The pieces were pierced to facilitate hanging, and gave

96 *(above) Porcelain bulb or bough pot.*
Sometimes termed a 'bouquetière'. The piece has a flat back and a semi-circular front. Painted in a brown monochrome with additional gilding, with an allegorical figure of an Indian girl representing America.
Height 4¾in, width 5⅜in. Mark: No 3 impressed, and the name 'America' painted. Date: c 1805-15.
Victoria and Albert Museum

97 *(below) Group of small decorative porcelain wares.*
Left: Small circular vase with frilled rim, set on three feet. Decorated with touches of gilding and an all-round scenic painting of a farmhouse and surrounding countryside.
Height 5in, diam 2⅝in. Mark: No 18 in red. Date: c 1870-80.
Hartley Asquith Esq

Centre: Miniature ink stand and cover. The body is in a low teapot shape with handle. There is a moulded spout-like holder for the quill. Set in the centre is an ink pot and cover. The body is decorated with enamelled and gilt scenes of birds, and on the reverse with a conventional rural scene of a church, cows, etc.
Height 2in, overall length 5in. Mark: No 16 printed in red. Date: c 1825-35.
Hartley Asquith Esq

Right: Pastille or incense burner in two pieces. The stand is set on four gilt feet and has an enamelled flower group on each edge, and on each top corner. The centre, beneath the cover, is pierced for air holes. The cover is conical and has three finely enamelled flower groups painted on the sides. It is surmounted by a gilt flame.
Overall height 5in. Mark: No 16 printed in red. Date: c 1820-30.

the impression of having been decorated by a professional at the factory.

A complete class of decorative Victorian china seems to be missing from the Davenport repertoire —parian ware. There is no reference to Davenport parian in the recently published study by D. and C. Schinn. Nor have my own extensive enquiries produced a single marked example. And yet, as has been noted on p 21, C. Shaw wrote of Davenport artists modelling parian when he worked at the factory in 1842. This is a suspiciously early date for parian in any factory, and may be a further example of Shaw being deliberately misleading about the identity of his oppressive employers. Certainly this evidence cannot stand alone. We can only express surprise that Davenports do not appear to have made parian and note that not a single marked piece has been located and this at a time—after 1840—when the vast majority of ware is marked. Unless they never marked such pieces one can go further and state that no figures of any kind, pottery, porcelain or parian, were made at Davenport. None have been recorded.

An interesting and attractive class of wares for collectors is represented in (98). Many printed souvenir mugs were made. In addition to the Lichfield cathedral piece, a slightly smaller mug printed with Gloucester cathedral and the legend 'a present from Gloucester', with the china dealer's mark, No 23, is in the author's collection. Other recorded subjects include 'Boscombe House, St Peter's Collegiate Church, Wolverhampton' with the dealer's name WALKER CHINA ROOMS W'HAMPTON (Sadler collection); 'St Mary's School Birkenhead' (on a saucer in the Williamson Art Gallery, Birkenhead); 'Primitive Methodist Jubilee Chapel Tunstall', dated 1860 (Hanley Museum); a very fine, coloured print of the 'Grand Parade Eastbourne' on a cup and saucer with the dealer's name GOSLING EASTBOURNE (Hanley Museum), and finally several examples of wares with prints of Hugh Bourne and William Clowes, the joint founders of the Primitive Methodists. This predeliction for the sect may have been for local and financial reasons, or possibly the more personal reason that Clowes is said to have served his apprenticeship at the Works and been one of Major John Davenport's Volunteers during the French wars (Jewitt, Vol II, p 284).

98 *(above left) Porcelain mug.*
Decorated on each side with an on-glaze print in black which is named 'Lichfield Cathedral'.
Height 3½in, diam 3½in. Mark: No 16 printed underglaze in blue. Date: c 1850-60.

99 *(above right) Porcelain jardinière.*
Heavily moulded ornamental jar and pierced cover, decorated with printed, enamelled and gilded Chinese scenes. On the front and back with different scenes of a man and a woman, on the sides with a flower group and a fish motif. In the narrow side panels, butterflies and flowers are enamelled in red and gilded.
Height 6¾in, width 4¾in. Mark: No 16 printed underglaze in blue. Date: c 1850-65.
Hanley Museum, Stoke-on-Trent

100 *(below) Porcelain plate.*
Decorated in a distinctive style and a subdued palette, with a scene of two soldiers at rest. The painting is signed 'E Lessore' on the front.
Diam 9in. Mark: No 16 printed underglaze in blue, and a painted monogram of a reversed 'E' and an 'L' in script. Date: c 1860.
Hanley Museum, Stoke-on-Trent

Lichfield Cathedral.

The plate (100) is a great rarity decorated by one of the truly individualistic ceramic artists of the Victorian period. Emile Lessore never—as far as is known—worked at Davenports. He came to England in 1858, worked briefly at Mintons, then moved to Wedgwoods which he left in 1863 to return to France. Here he continued to decorate Wedgwood—and obviously at least one Davenport piece—until his death in 1876 (see Alison Kelly, *Proceedings of the Wedgwood Society*, No 8, 1970, pp 260-2). This unique example does not constitute a case for regarding him as a Davenport artist.

Finally, attention must be drawn to the 'Japan' patterns as illustrated in (101 and 102). This was a most popular type of decoration in the last decade or so of the factory's existence. Such wares are not uncommon and may be found in a wide variety of forms ranging from dessert and breakfast wares as illustrated, to vases similar in form to the Coalport piece illustrated in Godden's *Victorian Porcelain*, plate 8. A large silver-mounted tray decorated with a Japan pattern number 4060 stands at one end of the scale to tiny salt cellars at the other. Some teaware shapes are illustrated in Godden's *Encyclopaedia*, plate 200. Other teawares have the hollow-ware pieces set upon three gilded feet. The list of wares, both useful and ornamental decorated in Japans, is very long indeed. The finish is every bit as good as that upon Crown Derby with which the Davenport specimens could so easily be confused. The last illustration (103) comes from Davenports Limited in the 1880s. As ever with the porcelain wares, good of its kind.

It has been impossible in the space available to do much more than hint at the wealth of wares produced at Longport. One is constantly meeting new shapes and new forms of decoration. The overall impression is of a conservative factory, not given to flights of fantasy or rash experimentation. The 'cash nexus' ruled the Davenports. They made what they knew they could sell. They gave no thought for the collector who, generations later, passes aesthetic judgment on their pots. Indeed, as we have seen, after the retirement of John Davenport, the principals of the firm knew little about and cared even less for the 'art and mystery' of potting. To make money, they paid people to make pots. The wonder is that so many of such wares afford pleasure to this day.

101 *(above left) Octagonal porcelain plate.*
Decorated with a traditional 'Japan' pattern in deep underglaze blue, and pink, red and green overglaze enamels with gilding.
Diam 9in. Mark: No 22 impressed and No 24 printed, pattern number 1931. Date: c 1880.

102 *(above right) Porcelain chocolate cup.*
One of a pair of small, double-handled chocolate cups with stands attached (covers missing). Decorated with a bold 'Japan' pattern and heavily gilt.
Height $3\frac{3}{4}$in, width $3\frac{3}{4}$in. Mark: No 18 printed in red, with letters 'N' in blue and 'O' in red, pattern number 6066 followed by three dots and '1'. Date: c 1880.
Hanley Museum, Stoke-on-Trent

103 *(below) Porcelain plates.*
Two moulded-edge plates decorated with enamel paintings of a bird and a country scene.
Diam 9in. Mark: No 22 impressed, no pattern number. A faded label on the bird plate is printed:
DAVENPORTS LIMITED
LONGPORT
SHAPE (not legible)
No. 45
Rate (not legible)
A further sale ticket records the price as '2gns' the pair. Date: 1881-7.
Hanley Museum, Stoke-on-Trent

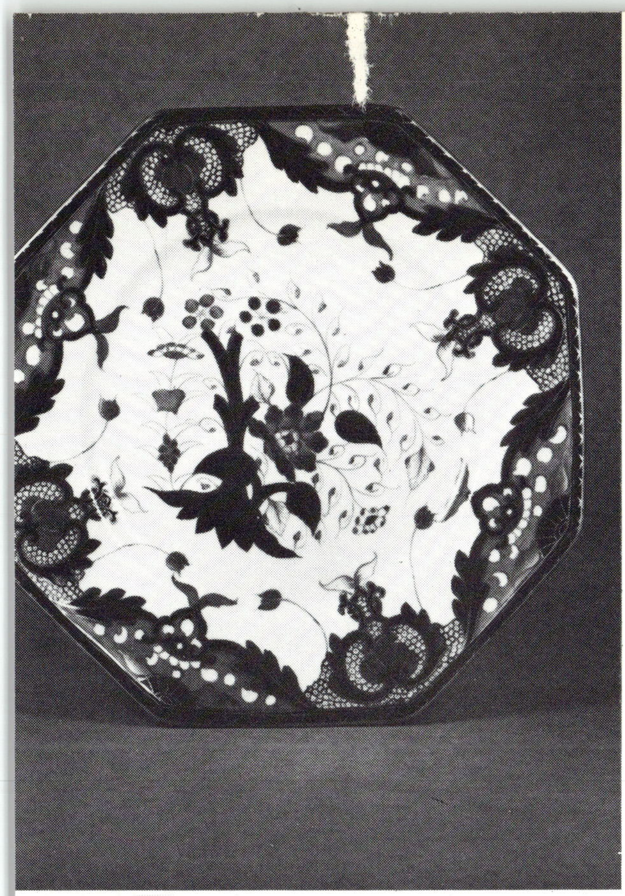

Marks on Earthenware (not to scale)

No 1 (IMPRESSED) Normally associated with the earliest earthenwares c 1795-1810. Occasionally found on porcelain pieces c 1820-40. See Godden, *Marks* p 708. Most porcelain with an anchor impressed is *not* Davenport but Coalport See Godden, *Coalport* p 18.

No 2 (IMPRESSED) In *lower case* letters, the early mark c 1798-1815. The distinction between this and No 3 is most important.

No 3 (IMPRESSED) In upper case letters a later mark than No 2, c 1815-60. Has been noted on certain porcelain pieces as exemplified in (96) and p 102.

No 4 (IMPRESSED) Similar to No 3 with date either side the anchor, here 1836. The system began c 1830 and was replaced by No 12 about 1860. The '6' impressed above is probably the month letter; thus June 1836.

No 5 (PRINTED) The very rare mark of the Henry and William Davenport partnership c 1832-5. See p 18 and (31) for details.

No 6 (PRINTED) An elaborate pattern-name mark found in association with No 7. See (36) also.

No 7 (PRINTED) Interesting mark of an American agent. See No 6 and also p 19 and (36) for details. The plate dates from 1836.

No 8 (PRINTED) A standard pattern-name mark with the firm's name added in capital letters. A great many variants of the basic mark with different pattern names have been recorded, some of which have been mentioned in the illustration captions. Such marks may date from c 1830-1887. Accurate dating is possible when the date marks No 4 or No 12 are also present. If absent, the style, decoration and shape have to be considered. 'Arabesque' is not illustrated, it dates from 1836.

No 9 (PRINTED) The most commonly found mark on stone china, usually in blue, rarely in red, c 1815-30.

No 10 (PRINTED) Usually in blue, less common than No 9. Dates from the same period c 1815-30. (Note: Godden *Marks* p 189 dates both No 9 and No 10 to c 1805. The evidence against this date for the introduction of stone china at Davenport's is given on p 60.)

No 11 (PRINTED) Rare mark in puce c 1820-40.

No 12 (IMPRESSED) Introduced when opaque china superseded stone china c 1850. Helpfully, it is usually accompanied by date numbers. Continued into the 1880s.

Marks on Porcelain (not to scale)

No 13 (PAINTED) The earliest porcelain mark, in red c 1800-15.

No 14 (PRINTED) A rather rare porcelain mark, usually in pale red overglaze, though also noted in green c 1810-20.

No 15a The words DAVENPORT / LONGPORT printed overglaze in green, puce or grey, have been noted on some early wares c 1810-20.

No 15b (PRINTED) The more usual version has STAFFORDSHIRE as the third line to No 15a. This latter version seems later c 1815-25.
Printed overglaze in puce or an unusual grey-pink shade.

No 16 (PRINTED) The most commonly found mark. There are two forms:
Printed *overglaze* in red, or more rarely brown. It is a comparatively early mark c 1815-30.
Printed *underglaze* in blue, the date is c 1845-75. This distinction is most important for accurately dating wares. Very occasionally the mark is in black, this seems to date from c 1850-70.

No 17 (PRINTED) A comparatively rare mark, printed overglaze in a pink-grey shade c 1830-40.

No 18 (PRINTED) Another very commonly encountered mark. Used in two quite distinct periods: Printed overglaze in a *pale puce* the date is c 1830-45. (Godden, *Marks*, p 191 does not note this early use of the mark he numbers 1194. But scores of specimens have been examined and confirm the earlier date when printed in this colour.) Printed overglaze in *red*. The mark is late c 1870-87.

No 19 (PRINTED) Overglaze in puce, the 'Royal' mark, 1830-37.

No 20 (PRINTED) Underglaze in blue with the design registration mark (here for 1849) and the factory name. Common on teawares c 1845-60.

No 21 (PRINTED) Overglaze in blue, a rare example of porcelain marked with a pattern name. This pattern c 1830-40.

No 22 (IMPRESSED) A late mark found on the porcelains c 1870-87. The letters are very small and the mark is often overlooked.

No 23 (PRINTED) A dealer's mark on a late piece c 1860-80. See p 106 for other examples.

No 24 (PRINTED) Another, and fairly common dealer's mark. Again dating from c 1875-87.

A number of other marks eg DAVENPORT'S / PATENT (see p 104) and DAVENPORTS LTD are noted in G. A. Godden, *Marks* p 191.

No 1

No 2

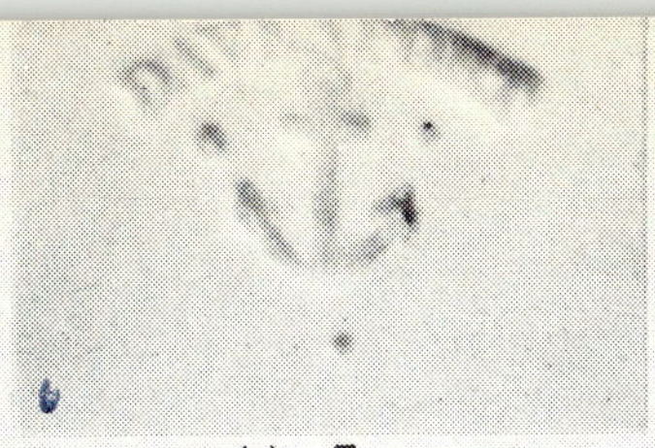
No 3

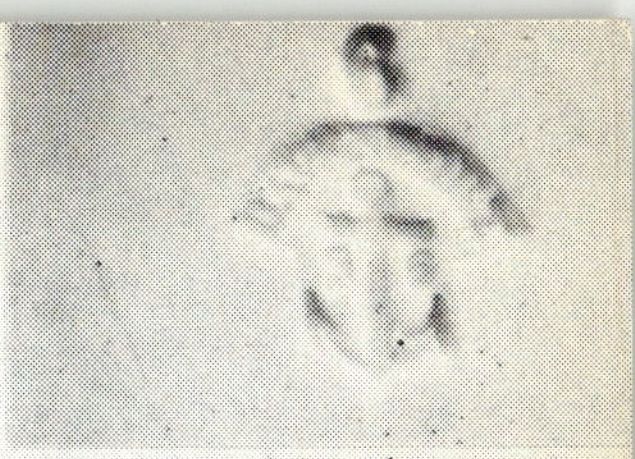
No 4

No 5

No 6

No 7

No 8

No 9

No 10

No 11

No 12

No 13

No 14

No 15

No 16

No 17

No 18

No 19

No 20

INDEX

(*numbers refer to pages*)